ALSO BY STEPHEN TEMPLIN

Special Operations Group Thrillers
Trident's First Gleaming: [#1]
From Russia Without Love: [#2]
Autumn Assassin: [#3]
(More books here: http://www.stephentemplin.com/books)

Special Operations Group Short Story
Dead in Damascus: [#0]

Nonfiction
Navy SEAL Training Class 144: My BUD/S Journal
SEAL Team Six: Memoirs of an Elite Navy SEAL Sniper (with Howard Wasdin)
I Am A SEAL Team Six Warrior (Young Adult version of *SEAL Team Six*)

Navy SEAL
Training Class 144

Navy SEAL Training Class 144
MY BUD/S JOURNAL

Stephen Templin

Some names and tactics have been changed to protect operators and their missions.
All Rights Reserved © 2015 by Stephen Templin
No part of this book may be reproduced or transmitted in any form or by any means, graphic, electronic, or mechanical, including photocopying, recording, taping, or by any information storage or retrieval system, without the written permission of the publisher.
Published by Stephen Templin
www.stephentemplin.com
ISBN-13: 9781518695049
ISBN-10: 1518695043
Cover design by Nuno Moreira. Photo courtesy of US Department of Defense.
Library of Congress Control Number: 2015917552
CreateSpace Independent Publishing Platform
North Charleston, South Carolina

EXCERPT OF *TRIDENT'S FIRST GLEAMING*
AT END OF THIS BOOK...

Author's Note

WHEN I FIRST BEGAN WRITING on Myspace about my experiences in Basic Underwater Demolition/SEAL (BUD/S) training, the response was incredible. People wanted more! In early 2009, I switched over to Facebook and continued writing there. Since then I've posted on a variety of social media platforms, including my website, which I've linked to close to a hundred thousand Twitter followers. Some of my training was completed with Howard E. Wasdin, and we shared some of these experiences in his biography, *SEAL Team Six: Memoirs of an Elite Navy SEAL Sniper*, read by nearly a million people—maybe more. Since then, I've received numerous requests to publish more about BUD/S training and my own experiences. Many read this for entertainment, some found inspiration, and others wanted to take their shot at becoming SEALs—one of my readers completed Hell Week! So here it is.

For those who are close to applying to BUD/S, I hope my story will be of some value to you, but you might want to take a quick look at the official Navy SEAL website at http://www.sealswcc.com to make sure you have the most accurate and up-to-date information for starting your journey. Next, you can skip to chapter 30, "Hell Week Survival Tips" for a summary of the critical value of self-efficacy (I wrote my PhD dissertation on this topic). Finally, the appendix at the end of this book provides some tips on navigating the official Navy SEAL website. Although my story may give you a strong feel for what BUD/S is like, and although a number of principles remain similar (for example, "The only easy day was yesterday" and "It pays to be a winner"), it's important to understand that BUD/S is constantly evolving. There are so many variables involved that it is unlikely that every class will be identical in every way—in one BUD/S class no one passed, and in another everyone graduated. In order for me to make it through Hell Week, I found it valuable to be, among other things, both prepared and flexible.

Warning

DO NOT TRY ANY OF the activities described here on your own. Even with the supervision and guidance of active-duty SEAL instructors, serious injuries have resulted. Without this experienced supervision and guidance, permanent injuries or death can result.

CHAPTER 1

Breakout—No Bell Hell Week

WHAT IF WE STOLE THE *bell before Hell Week?* When a Basic Underwater Demolition/SEAL (BUD/S) trainee has had enough, he is supposed to ring a bell to signal he's quitting. More students drop out of training during Hell Week than any other time, but my class was determined not to lose a single classmate during the infamous week.

In our barracks on the beach of Coronado, California, our class met in the lounge, and we hatched a plan to steal the bell. We elected one of our ninjas to do the deed, and then he was to hand it off to the guy voted least likely to quit Hell Week, who would stash it somewhere and not tell a soul where it was. We were always looking for a competitive edge—playing the game in a way that favored us. It was important to think ahead as to what the consequences of such actions might be, but it was also important to play the game with guts.

That evening, some of us slept while others remained awake in their beds. Wearing my Battle Dress Uniform (BDUs) and combat boots in preparation for Hell Week, I slept soundly in my rack. I awoke to the sound of a metal *click* in the head (restroom). My room was black, except for the sudden flash of an M60 machine gun blasting from inside the head. The noise assaulted my ears. I saw my classmates crawling out the door, so I crawled out with them.

"Move, move, move!" an instructor yelled.

Outside on the grinder (an asphalt area used for exercise, drills, and other activities), artillery simulators exploded in the night air—an incoming shriek followed by a *boom*. More machine guns rattled off, a fog machine pumped a blanket of mist over the ground, and green ChemLights decorated the outer perimeter. Then water hoses sprayed us as a swarm of instructors descended. An instructor blew his whistle. *Tweet*—whistle drill. We dove to the ground, crossed our legs, covered our ears, and opened our mouths as if preparing for an explosion to ensure legs wouldn't be torn off and our ears wouldn't rupture. I could smell cordite in the air. I loved the odor. To me, it smelled like excitement. This was Breakout, the beginning of Hell Week.

Tweet, tweet. We low-crawled to the sound of the whistle. *Tweet, tweet, tweet.* We stood up.

The whistle drills continued between the explosions and the chatter of machine guns. Each time the whistle blew twice, I crawled toward the sound, the asphalt rubbing the skin off my knees and elbows. Of the three whistle sounds, I quickly learned to hate the double tweet more than a single or triple. Finally the whistle blew three times and we stood up.

Instructor Blah stood on a platform, calmly speaking into the bullhorn. "Get in formation!" We hurried into a formation of boat crews.

"On your backs! On your feet! On your stomachs!" The commands were too fast, nearly impossible to follow.

"You people are not working together! Drop and push 'em out!" We did push-ups.

"Give me a muster, Mr. Mark," Instructor Blah said.

The artillery simulators and machine guns filled the air with thunder.

"Boat leaders, report!" shouted our class officer, Mr. Mark.

With the sounds of the shooting, artillery, and screaming, it was challenging for us to communicate. My boat crew and I counted off and reported to our boat leader. He and the other boat leaders reported to Mr. Mark. "All present, sir!"

"Any day now, Mr. Mark," Instructor Blah said.

"All present," Mr. Mark reported.

Instructor Blah raised his eyebrows. "All present?"

"Yes. All present, Instructor Blah."

"Drop!" Blah said in the megaphone.

We all dropped to the push-up position.

"You people have given me a false muster!" Instructor Blah's voice kept the same monotone. "One of your men is missing!"

Not moving from the push-up position, Mr. Mark said, "Boat leaders, give me a muster!"

The explosions and machine-gun fire became louder. Maintaining the push-up position, my boat leader walked on his hands to each of us to make sure all of us were present.

One of the other boat crew leaders reported, "Seaman Nelson is missing, sir!"

Mr. Mark reported, "Seaman Nelson is missing, Instructor Blah."

"First you told me all present! Now you tell me Seaman Nelson is missing! Which is it?"

"Seaman Nelson is missing, sir!" Ensign Mark said.

Three instructors brought out Seaman Nelson, took off his blindfold, gag, and plasticuffs. Seaman Nelson returned to his boat crew. "The instructors kidnapped me," he said. In all the noise and confusion of Breakout, no one had noticed he'd been missing.

Instructor Blah calmly said, "No SEAL has ever been kept as a prisoner of war. But you left Seaman Nelson behind, didn't you? Push 'em out!"

We did push-ups until our arms gave out. Then we did calisthenics. During the jumping jacks, the senior chief SEAL sprayed a water hose inches from my face, directly up my nose.

I counted off as best I could. "One, two, three, one! One, two, three, two!" My words became more and more gargled, and I gagged a couple of times. I was happy to be out of the push-up position and delighted not to be doing whistle drills, but I hid my emotions. No pain, no joy. Eventually, the senior chief became bored and moved on to harass someone else.

Tweet. Prostrated body, crossed legs, covered ears, opened mouths.

Tweet, tweet. Low-crawl. *Tweet, tweet.* Low-crawl. Our bloody knees and elbows dragged across the merciless blacktop. As we neared the beach, I sped up so I could crawl on the soft sand instead of the asphalt. When I realized where we were headed—the cold ocean—I slowed down, not in a hurry to get wet. I had to be careful not to go too slow and receive special attention from the instructors. *Stay with the group.*

We moved farther and farther from the chaotic sounds of instructors shouting, machine guns shooting, and artillery shells exploding behind us. Most of the instructors had faded away, and only a handful remained.

Hell Week had barely begun, and we already appeared ragged, like hunted animals scraping to survive. We crawled on our hands and knees until we eventually reached the waterline.

Instructor Blah held the megaphone up to his lips. "Prepare for surf torture!"

"Hooyah!" we shouted in unison. I don't know where the sudden burst of spirit came from, but it lifted us. We formed a line, facing the instructors, and we locked arms.

"You have something that belongs to the instructors, and we want it back!" Instructor Blah said.

At that moment, we were the proudest we'd ever been as a class. The instructors thought they could break us, but we believed they couldn't. We were in control. We had something they wanted, and they weren't going to get it. "Hooyah!"

"Take three steps backwards and sit down!"

"Hooyah!" Our voices shouted louder than ever. Arms locked, we sat down in frigid water up to our necks, but the water didn't seem so cold. We were fighting back.

"You give us the bell, and the instructors will take it easier on you! You don't give us the bell, and this is going to be the worst Hell Week ever!"

We remained defiant. "Hooyah!" Waves of water crashed over us.

"You have stolen government property! That's a federal offense!" The more Instructor Blah asked for the bell, the more our spirits shot into outer space.

"Hooyah!" we called out, as if flipping our middle fingers. Some of us were laughing.

"You will all end up in the brig if you don't return our bell!"

Sitting there in the water, my classmates and I responded by breaking out in song to the tune of "Take Me Out to the Ball Game."

Take me out to the surf zone.
Take me out to the sea.
Make me do push-ups and jumping jacks.
I don't care if I never get back.
For it's root, root, root for the SEAL teams.
If we don't pass, it's a shame.
For it's one, two, three rings you're out
Of the old BUD/S game!

"Hooyah!" we shouted merrily.

The instructors quietly conferred with one another as we sat in water up to our chests. Each successive wave hammered us, sapping the warmth from our bodies and push-pulling at our locked arms. Our butts scraped forward and back across broken seashells and rocks. We started to shiver, and our arms began to weaken.

"If you quit now, you can have a blanket and a hot cup of cocoa . . . with marshmallows," Instructor Blah said calmly in the megaphone.

I retreated into my own private world of cold and pain. The hush among my classmates told me that they were doing the same. We shorter guys sat deeper in the water than the others. Petty Officer Lin, a Ranger veteran who'd fought in Grenada, who had completed half of Hell Week in an earlier class, shivered more than anyone.

The waves began to break our human chain. Soon, most of us were separated. I knew this couldn't go on forever. I knew the instructors had carefully calculated the air temperature, water temperature, and wind speed, so they knew the maximum amount of time they could expose us to the cold without killing us. Physically, I could survive this. I just had to endure the pain mentally.

The instructors wanted their bell, and we weren't going to give it to them. The battle of wills had only just begun.

CHAPTER 2

The Journey of a Thousand Miles

THE JOURNEY OF A THOUSAND miles begins with the first step, and I stepped into the navy to become a SEAL because I wanted to fight with some of the best against terrorists. In 1985, most Americans knew little about SEALs or terrorism, but I'd already read a lot about the SEALs' actions in Vietnam and current terrorism threats (at the time) around the globe. During boot camp at Great Lakes, Illinois, I got my chance to take the physical screen test (PST)—the gateway to BUD/S training.

This was the moment I'd been working toward. We started out with the swim, my Achilles' heel. And I failed.

Do not go to BUD/S training. Do not pass go. Do not collect $200.

I was devastated, but I picked myself up and recommitted to accomplishing my goal, trying to make the best of the situation. I ended up stationed on a ship in Long Beach,

California. I chipped paint and swabbed decks for months. On the upside, I got to visit places like the Philippines and Hong Kong. I even worked extra hours to become an apprentice hospital corpsman—similar to an army medic.

When our ship was in port, the navy had good pools (something I didn't have regular access to growing up), and I trained in them often. Each week I swam in the ocean bay with fins, and every day I ran and did push-ups, sit-ups, and chin-ups. When our ship was sailing, I couldn't practice swimming, ironically, but I could jog around on the flight deck and work out in the weight room. I did everything I could to get in better shape.

Months later, two other guys on my ship, Rudy and Claude, decided they wanted to be SEALs, too, so we trained together. Then one day they walked into the gym with big smiles on their faces.

"The PST is tomorrow," Rudy announced. "Let's do it."

"I'm not ready yet," I said. "I'm going to Hospital Corpsman School, then will be assigned to a Marine unit for a while. By then I'll be in shape and try again."

But they wouldn't let me out of it that easy. "What've you got to lose?" Claude asked. "The worst thing that could happen is you fail."

So the next day I went with them to take the PST on base. After showing our IDs and paperwork, we stripped down to our swim shorts. "All you have to do now is swim five hundred yards in eight and a half minutes using the sidestroke or breaststroke," a Navy SEAL reminded us.

I was nervous to say the least. At the sound of the whistle, we swam. I used the breaststroke, but after about 250 yards I grew tired and switched to the sidestroke. I had no technique whatsoever—just went as fast as I could from beginning to end. As I approached the end of the swim, the clock neared our deadline: eight minutes and twenty-seven seconds, twenty-eight, twenty-nine . . . I finished with only one second remaining.

I was both excited and shocked that I'd passed the first hurdle. Others hadn't passed. For those of us who remained, including Rudy and Claude, we changed into T-shirts, long pants, and boots.

"You have to do thirty-five push-ups in two minutes and thirty-five sit-ups in two minutes," the SEAL said. I did more than forty of each. One guy—Muscleman—did a lot more. But three of the candidates were sent walking.

"Next, you have to do six pull-ups from a dead hang. The time limit is over when you fall from the bar." After exerting myself on the swim, push-ups, and sit-ups, I only had enough energy to do eight pull-ups. Muscleman did twelve. My buddies were still with me, but two more candidates failed.

The last part of the test was the run, wearing pants and boots. "You will run a mile and a half in eight and a half minutes. Good luck."

At the sound of the whistle, Muscleman took off like a horse from a starting gate. I knew I couldn't keep up with him, and I ran at my own careful pace. At about halfway, I passed Muscleman and some others. I crossed the finish line in under seven minutes. Two candidates were too slow—Muscleman was one of them. Out of the sixteen of us who had started, only eight of us passed the physical screening test, including me, Rudy, and Claude. But we still had to pass the dental and medical exams, and the hyperbaric chamber test.

CHAPTER 3

Inspected, Injected & Selected

I N ORDER TO BE ACCEPTED to BUD/S training, I had to take my dental, medical, and psychological exam at the Naval Hospital in Long Beach. The dentist poked around in my mouth, took X-rays, and even cleaned my teeth—not a single cavity. The medical exam wasn't so different from civilian medical exams I'd taken: weight, height, blood, urine, eyes, ears, heart, chest, and "Turn your head and cough." The medical staff also made sure my immunizations were up-to-date: typhoid, tetanus, yellow fever, hepatitis A, flu, and PPD.

My vision checked out better than 20/40 in one eye and 20/70 in the other. But when they tested my color vision with the FALANT (Farnsworth lantern) test, a test using colored lights, I failed. Fortunately, there was a mix-up with the paperwork, and I still got a pass mark. (Although I couldn't pass the FALANT, I've never had a problem properly identifying colored lights, flares, tracer rounds, and so on. Also, I'm more sensitive to shapes than colors, so sometimes I can more easily spot camouflaged personnel and objects.)

I had been inspected, injected, and selected. A doctor looked over my paperwork and gave his stamp of approval. About ten other guys weren't as lucky.

Later, I took the psychology questionnaire. It asked me the same questions over and over. I wasn't sure whether they were checking the reliability of the test or my patience in doing this. One question was "Do you want to be a fashion designer?" I didn't know whether fashion designers were crazy, or whether I was crazy for not wanting to be one.

It also asked, "Do you have thoughts about suicide?" I didn't have thoughts about it before the test, but after answering so many questions about suicide, I started to consider it!

"Do you like *Alice in Wonderland*?" *How should I know? I never read it.*

The prophet Moses would have failed the test questions "Have you had visions?" and "Do you have special abilities?" After the paper test, I was more than happy to meet with the psychiatrist, tell her what she wanted to hear, and finally pass.

Next, I went in for my hyperbaric pressure testing.[1] The chamber was a large torpedo-like thing. I was fortunate to see the candidate before me taking his test, so I knew what to

---

[1] Hyperbaric chamber testing is no longer currently done in the Navy SEALs screen test. Also, on the concept of controlling stress through meditation, as of this writing, I am told that BUD/S teaches "four and four for four": Breathe in for four seconds, exhale for four seconds, and repeat for four minutes. This should help you relax through stressful situations. I didn't have the luxury of this technique when I went through my testing, but I would

expect. While I was filling out my paperwork, the candidate stepped into the hyperbaric chamber and sat down. I could see him through the window, sweating before the dive operator told him he was dropping the pressure. When the operator simulated ten feet underwater, the candidate's face turned red.

At twenty feet, the dive officer asked the candidate via telecom, "Everything okay?"

"Of course it's not okay. Let me out!"

I don't know if it was the claustrophobia, the air pressure, or both, but the candidate didn't stick around. Fail.

Then it was my turn. I stepped inside, sat down, and relaxed. I'd practiced meditation before, so I slowed my breathing and heartbeat to calm myself. The dive officer sealed the door shut on me. I went down ten feet, twenty feet. I could feel the air pressure increasing. At thirty feet, I was already yawning and swallowing in order to relieve some of the pressure on my ears. Now the chamber was simulating what it'd be like sixty feet underwater and stayed there. No problem.

After ten minutes at sixty feet, the dive officer slowly relieved the pressure inside my chamber until it was gone.

"Good job," he said.

I was told that usually only one out of about a hundred guys make it to the stage in the selection process I had reached. It felt good to make it this far. At that point, I really didn't know what was around the corner for me at BUD/S training, but ignorance was happiness, and I was ecstatic!

---

often breathe deep and exhale long until I calmed myself through a stressful moment.

CHAPTER 4

Vietnam SEAL Mentor

I ARRIVED AT THE NAVAL Special Warfare Center in Coronado, California, to begin BUD/S training on December 31, 1986. With SEAL instructors and staff still out for the holidays, I slipped in mostly unnoticed. I could've reported a couple of days later, but I was too anxious. Luckily, on Friday, January 2, 1987, SEAL master chief Rick Knepper helped me shake off the nerves by volunteering to help me and other early arrivals get a leg up on training.

Knepper looked like an ordinary guy in his forties, and he calmly led us in calisthenics on the beach late in the afternoon. We grunted and groaned, but he didn't seem to break a sweat. He'd served in Vietnam with SEAL Team One, Delta Platoon, Second Squad. Knepper's squad knew about Hon Toi, a large island in Nha Trang Bay, but they didn't know enemies were there. From a distance, the island had looked like a big rock sitting in the ocean for birds to take a crap on. But two Vietcong (VC), tired of fighting and being away from family, had defected from the island, leaving a VC camp behind.

Knepper and seven teammates then inserted into the island by boat under the cover of darkness—not even the moon shone. Never ones to take the easy way, they free-climbed a 350-foot cliff. After reaching the top, they lowered themselves into the VC camp. The seven-man squad split into two fire teams, taking off their boots and going barefoot to search for some high-value targets (HVTs) to snatch. But the VC got the drop on one fire team, led by Lieutenant (junior grade) Bob Kerrey. A grenade landed at his feet and exploded, slamming him into the rocks and destroying the lower half of his leg. The lieutenant's fire team fought back while he called on his teammates for help, catching the VC in a deadly crossfire. One SEAL, a hospital corpsman, lost his eye. Four of the enemy tried to escape, but the SEALs cut them down. Three VC stayed to fight, but none lived to fight another battle.

One of the SEALs wrapped a tourniquet around Lieutenant Kerrey's leg as the rest of the squad snatched several HVTs along with three large bags of documents—later found to include a list of VC in the city—weapons, and other equipment. Lieutenant Kerrey continued to lead Knepper and the others in his squad until they were evacuated. In the end, the intel they procured from the documents and HVTs provided critical information to the allied forces in Vietnam. Lieutenant Kerrey received the Medal of Honor, and after leaving the navy, he went on to become the thirty-fifth governor of Nebraska and a US senator.

Although others still talk about that op, I never heard Master Chief Knepper talk about it or any other. He served as a mentor to me and my classmates, and without his taking us under his wing, we would've been left on our own until the rest of the guys arrived and our BUD/S class officially formed. And I was going to need all the help I could get.

CHAPTER 5

Good News, Bad News

WHEN CLASS 143 FINALLY BEGAN BUD/S Indoctrination (Indoc), I found out that we would be taking the physical screen test again. I nearly panicked hearing that those who failed would be dropped on the spot. But the fear must've motivated me because I passed while others were sent packing.

From that point on, it took everything I had to get through the calisthenics of Indoc without being targeted by the instructors for not keeping up. During the pool swims, I always finished dead last. Guys already started to ring the bell—quitting.

The beach runs hammered me. Soft sand sucked the energy out of my legs, but waves assaulted me on the hard-packed sand. Some guys dropped way behind, and others stayed in front with the group. I ran with the guys strung out in the middle.

One day, Instructor Benelli ran alongside me. "Do you want to fall behind with the guys walking in the back, or keep up with the guys running in front?"

I gasped. "Front."

"Run with your thighs and not your lower legs, then. Just pick up your thighs and put them down. Keep your arms loose so you don't waste energy. And *breathe*."

I followed his advice and somehow managed to make my way forward. My former shipmate, Rudy, stayed strong like Clint Eastwood and was almost always up front, giving me someone to catch up to. Other guys, like Howard E. Wasdin, whom I met and became friends with in Indoc, fell behind on one run and received personal attention from the instructors while the rest of us hit the showers. In Howard's case, he would never make that mistake again. In contrast, Claude seemed to fall farther behind on every run. I couldn't understand why. Claude and I had run together before BUD/S, and he'd never had trouble. But I noticed he didn't smile anymore. One day he rang the bell, and I never saw him again.

After one particularly tough day of training, Howard walked around the barracks asking, "Who wants to go with me for a run on the beach?"

I thought he was nuts. "You're in BUD/S. Isn't that enough?" What seemed even nuttier to me was that some of the guys actually went.

Howard set a positive example for me in BUD/S and was a great friend.[2] But when I injured a leg muscle trying

---

2 Years later, in 1993, in Mogadishu, Somalia, Howard and three other snipers from SEAL Team Six, along with Delta and others, snatched some of warlord Mohamed Aidid's top cadre. Aidid's militia used rocket-propelled grenades to shoot down two Black Hawk helicopters. Howard and his

to swim with my hands and feet tied while preparing for "drownproofing," that was the end of our training together. The doctors pulled me out of Class 143.

The bad news was that I had to start Indoc all over from the very beginning. But the good news was that I was still in the game. I'd gotten a taste of BUD/S, and I was determined to hook up with Class 144 and kick some ass.

---

buddies fought a hellish battle to get out of the city. The rest of Howard's story appears in *SEAL Team Six: Memoirs of an Elite Navy SEAL Sniper*.

CHAPTER 6

Starting Over

ALTHOUGH MY INJURY WAS SERIOUS enough to roll me back in training, it wasn't debilitating enough to take me completely out. I trained harder than ever as I recovered and entered Class 144 faster and stronger than I'd been before.

At 0500 on the first day of Class 144's Indoc, we sat shivering, wearing only our Underwater Demolition Team (UDT) swim shorts, on the cold concrete next to the pool officially known as the Combat Training Tank. The sky was black, but lights illuminated the pool.

One of our instructors, a man named John Stoneclam, walked into the pool area, his eyes wide and crazed in a scary, unpredictable way.

Ensign Mark was our class leader, a graduate from MIT, so it was his responsibility to get us moving.[3] "Feet!" Mark shouted.

---

[3] Years later, as a SEAL officer, he would lead Howard E. Wasdin and their SEAL Team Two platoon in Iraq.

We jumped to attention.

"Feet!" he yelled again. "Instructor Stoneclam!" Ensign Mark said.

"Hooyah, Instructor Stoneclam!" our class greeted him.

Instructor Stoneclam coldly surveyed us. "Some of you guys are shivering. Let me warm you up a bit. Drop."

"Drop!" Mark repeated.

We each scrambled to find an empty place on the concrete to get in the push-up position.

"Push 'em out," Instructor Stoneclam said.

After three sets of twenty push-ups, we took the same PST as I'd done before: swimming, push-ups, sit-ups, pull-ups, and running. Only this time, I wasn't the slowest during the swim. Martinez, one of my new roommates, was. Martinez and our other roommate, Duque, had come from La Infanteria de Marina, Ecuador's marine commandos. I'd heard people say that BUD/S training is the toughest in the world, but La Infanteria de Marina training was so brutal that one of their classmates had died.

One of our guys failed the PST, and the instructors sent him to pack his sea bag.

CHAPTER 7

Rocket's Red Glare

On another morning, at about 0500, we stood on the beach in formation waiting to begin physical training (PT). It was too dark to see the ocean behind us, but we could hear the waves. Outdoor lights illuminated our barracks, and the Naval Special Warfare Center in front of us. We sang "The *Star-Spangled Banner*." I thought we were doing a pretty good job, despite singing off-key and forgetting the words, but Martinez, Duque, and our two Egyptian officers were just botching it. The four foreign guys were trying their best, but it only got worse. Some members of our class started snickering.

Suddenly, I heard a *thunk* from behind, and a classmate came flying forward like he'd been shot out of an artillery cannon. He crashed into the guy in front of him, and the two of them tumbled to the sand.

A voice came out from the darkness behind us. "What is so funny about 'The *Star-Spangled Banner*'?"

"Instructor Stoneclam!" Ensign Mark shouted.

Instructor Stoneclam cut us off. "Shut up and drop!"

We dropped to the push-up position and waited in silence. I thought the days of military instructors hitting trainees were over, but I'd thought wrong. Now I was nervous. It wasn't the kind of nervousness you'd have wandering in a dark alley at night, worried you'd be attacked by a street thug. It was more the kind of fear you'd have waiting to be attacked by a Navy SEAL in the dark. Because that's exactly what had happened.

Instructor Stoneclam marched to the front of our formation and faced us. His eyes were on fire. "I want to know what is funny about 'The Star-Spangled Banner'! Is it the bombs bursting in air? The rockets' red glare?"

No answer.

"Is the flag funny? I want to know what is so damn funny about our national anthem!"

"Nothing is funny about the national anthem, Instructor Stoneclam," Ensign Mark said.

Instructor Stoneclam nodded. "You got that right. Push 'em out!"

After we finished the first set of twenty push-ups, he stopped us in the up position, also known as a "front leaning rest," as we were waiting for permission to recover.

"Push 'em out!"

Nope. We weren't getting that permission yet.

Over one hundred push-ups later, our arms and legs were trembling. Our sagging bodies had to strain to stay off the ground.

"Get wet and sandy!" he commanded.

We sprinted to the ocean, dove in, hurried out of the water, and rolled ourselves in the soft sand until we basically looked like sugar cookies. Somehow the sand had found its way into my eyes, ears, nose, mouth, and crack of my ass. The sand may have looked like sugar, but it sure didn't taste like it. And the sand didn't dissolve the way sugar did when it got wet. It rubbed like sandpaper.

"Full jumping jacks. Ready, begin," Instructor Stoneclam called.

Our class sounded off. "One, two, three, four—one. One, two, three, four—two . . ."

Instructor Stoneclam did the PT with us, leading from the front as all the SEAL instructors did. When we finished, we were like giant jellyfish there on the sand. And, although our laughing was the issue, we never sang "The *Star-Spangled Banner*" again during training.

CHAPTER 8

Super Marios

L IKE MARIO IN A NINTENDO video game, you can hit the obstacle course running, jumping, and ducking. But unlike Mario, you *will* feel the pain. The sun shone brightly as we stood in formation on the beach south of our barracks where the obstacle course—affectionately known as the O-Course—was set up.

A SEAL instructor stood in front of us. "Some night you might have to lock out of a submarine, hang on to your life as your Zodiac jumps over waves, scale a cliff, hump through enemy territory to your objective, scale a three-story building, do your business, and get out. The O-Course is going to help you do all that.

"Remember that when you get to the Slide for Life," he went on, "if you think you're going to fall, hang on to the rope with your hands. Let go of your feet first, then release your hands and fall. Doc is here, but don't expect him to put Humpty Dumpty back together if you land on your head and paralyze yourself."

After the instructor demonstrated the whole course, we lined up in alphabetical order by last name. I was near the end, and when my turn came, I took off like a chimp with hemorrhoids. I found the most effective strategy was to use my legs and reserve my arms for balance. The thighs are the biggest muscles in the body, so it pays to take advantage of that.

Toward the end of the parallel bars I used my arms to spring me forward and up, then slapped the end of the bars as I came down, saving a fraction of a second. Next, I ran full speed at the low wall (twelve feet was considered low). Still running, I leaped up and landed on a stump with my right foot first. I jumped from the stump like Mario and caught the top of the wall with my stomach, and my momentum flipped me over to the other side.

I sprinted to the high wall and climbed the rope. The guy next to me tried to climb his rope straight up, but he lost his footing and fell back down. I kept my body low and perpendicular to the wall, passing him. Then I belly-crawled under the barbed wire, passing another classmate.

After the crawl was the sixty-foot cargo net. I pumped my legs, stepping up the horizontal ropes, while I used my hands on one of the vertical ropes to guide me up. The outer edges of the net were closer to the poles suspending it, making the rope there firmer and easier to climb. The rope in the middle sagged and took more energy and balance to conquer. When I reached the top rail of the cargo net, I stretched an arm over the top and down to the other side, where I grabbed a handful of rope. I flipped myself over the net. At about sixty feet above the ground, it was far from the safest technique, but it was the fastest. Going down, I used my arms like a gorilla, grabbing the lowest horizontal rope I could reach with one hand, then dropping down while my other hand reached for the next lowest handhold. I passed another classmate.

Next, I carefully steadied myself over the balance logs. One of my classmates fell off and was just starting over as I passed him, too.

I double-timed over the next part of the O-Course, a pyramid of logs called the Hooyah Logs.

After that, I ran to the rope transfer. I grabbed as high up the rope as I could and lifted my legs into a squatting position. I wrapped the rope around my right leg, beginning from between my thighs, crossing over the back of my calf, coming around the outside of my ankle, and laying the rope across the top of my right boot. With my left boot, I stepped on top of the rope, clamping it between the bottom of my left boot and the top of my right boot. I stood and stretched until my hands could grab higher on the rope. Then I loosened the rope on my right leg and again raised my legs into a squatting position. Then I wrapped the rope around my right leg, stood, and stretched. I continued this routine up the rope like an inchworm. It wasn't a fast technique, but it conserved arm energy. When I reached the top, I grabbed a second rope, positioned next to the one I'd climbed, then slid down it. I'd wrapped my right leg around the rope to slow my descent and save me from a crashing into the ground.

Then came the Dirty Name. It deserved its reputation, with its horizontal logs spaced at devious intervals. I jumped from one to the next. I almost jumped too high and too far, nearly clearing the log and falling headfirst into the sand. Then I jumped to the next one. This time, I jumped high enough, but my jump almost wasn't far enough. I somehow managed to wiggle over the top and drop down on the other side.

I double-timed over another pyramid of Hooyah Logs.

Next, I hit the Weaver. Like a human needle and thread, I sewed myself in and out of a series of parallel pipes that ascended and descended in the shape of a stretched-out triangle.

Then I climbed a rope about twelve feet up to the Burma Bridge, strategically using my legs more than my arms. I quickly walked across the seventy-five-foot rope bridge and lowered myself down the rope on the other end.

Next, I ran to the bottom of a three-story tower. At the top, a rope stretched about one hundred feet across to a low bar. But there were no ropes or ladders to climb up the three-story tower. Instead, I had to jump to grab the second-story ledge, then swing my legs up—repeating the process up to the third level. From the top, I climbed across the hundred-foot rope, also known as the "Slide for Life." I started by using the commando style—pulling myself across the top of the rope while my body faced down—but I lost my balance and ended up under the rope, staring up at the sky. Fortunately, I hadn't let go; I was just hanging there like a pig tied to a spit. My ad-libbed "banana style" used up more of my arm strength than the commando style, but at that point I was more worried about finishing before I fell off and broke my neck.

One of my classmates—I think it was Petty Officer Tee—who was behind me wasn't so lucky. He had used up his arm strength on many of the obstacles and got stuck, banana style, crossing the Slide for Life.

"Feetfirst!" Doc, one of our SEAL instructors, yelled. "Fall feetfirst!"

But Tee had no energy in his arms to do anything except lock them on to the rope and hope he didn't die. Soon his arm lock broke, and he fell about six feet. His body fizzled to the earth, and his alien-shaped, buzz-cut head landed in the sand, his feet almost straight up in the air.

Doc sprinted over to him. The drab olive-green 4WD medical truck arrived behind him.

Tee stood up and brushed the sand out of his hair stubble. He looked more embarrassed than hurt.

"Sit down," Doc said.

Tee sat.

Doc looked into Tee's eyes. "What is your name?"

"Petty Officer Tee."

"Where are you?"

"The O-Course."

An instructor brought out the litter, what we called a "basketlike stretcher."

"You seem okay, but we're going to have Medical take a look at you to make sure," Doc said.

Navy SEAL Training Class 144

The instructors strapped Tee into the litter, loaded him in the ambulance, and took him away. Later, we found out that he was okay. And that I had set the class record for the O-Course.

CHAPTER 9

Surf Passage

Instructor Stoneclam stood next to a thirteen-foot-long black rubber boat resting on the floor in front of me and my fellow trainees in a classroom at the Naval Special Warfare Center.

"Today, I'm going to brief you on Surf Passage. This is the IBS. Some people call it the 'itty-bitty ship,' and you'll probably come up with your own pet names to give it, but the navy calls it the 'inflatable boat, small.' You will man it with six to eight men, all who are about the same height as you. These men will be your boat crew."

On the board, he drew a primitive picture of the beach, ocean, and stickmen scattered around the IBS. He pointed to the stickmen. "This is you guys after a wave has just wiped you out." Then he drew a stickman on the beach. "This is one of you after the ocean spit you out. And guess what? The next thing the ocean is going to spit out is the boat."

Instructor Stoneclam used his eraser as the boat. "But now the one-hundred-seventy-pound IBS is full of water and weighs about as much as a small car. And it's coming right at you here on the beach. What are you going to do? If you're standing in the road and a small car comes speeding at you, what do you do? Try to outrun it? Of course not. You're going to get out of the road. Same thing when the boat comes speeding at you. You're going to get out of the path it's traveling. Run parallel to the beach."

He looked around the room at us. "Hmm. Some of you look sleepy. All of you drop and push 'em out!"

Later that day, the sunshine faded as we stood by our boats facing the ocean. Bulky orange kapok life jackets covered our Battle Dress Uniforms (BDUs). We tied our hats to the top buttonholes on our shirt collars with orange cord. We held our paddles like rifles at the order-arms position, waiting for our boat crew leaders to return from where the instructors briefed them.

My group was the "Smurf Crew"—the boat with the shortest men—and when our boat leader returned, he quickly gave us orders. With boat handle in one hand and paddle in the other, we raced into the water. The other boat crews did the same.

"One's in!" our boat leader called. Our two front men jumped into the boat and started paddling.

"Two's in!"

I ran into the water almost up to my knees. Martinez and I jumped in and started paddling.

"Three's in!" the boat leader called. The third pair jumped in and paddled, followed by our boat leader, who sat at the stern and used his oar to steer.

"Stroke, stroke!"

I dug my paddle in deep and pulled back as hard as I could. I glanced over at another boat, where one of our Egyptian exchange officers had a big smile on his face, as if he were on the Catalina Island cruise. His paddle leisurely slapped the top of the water.

In front of us, a seven-foot wave formed.

"Dig, dig, dig!" our boat leader shouted.

Our boat climbed up the face of the wave as the boat beside us cleared the tip. That wasn't to be our destiny. The wave picked us up and slammed us down, sandwiching men between the boat and the water. As the ocean ate us, I ate a mouthful of boots, paddles, and cold saltwater.

Eventually, the ocean regurgitated us onto the beach, along with most of the other boat crews. The instructors greeted us by dropping us. With our boots on the boats, hands in the sand, and gravity against us, we did push-ups.

Then we gathered ourselves together and went at it again—with more motivation and better teamwork. This time, we cleared the breaking waves.

I glanced back at the shore, where a boyish-faced trainee from another boat crew was picking his paddle up off the beach. As he turned around to face the ocean, a rogue boat full of water and no passengers raced sideways at him.

"Get out of there!" Instructor Stoneclam shouted into the megaphone.

Boy-Face ran away from the boat, just as the instructors had told us not to. Fear has a way of turning Einsteins into amoebas.

"Run parallel to the beach! Run parallel to the beach!"

Boy-Face continued to try to outrun the speeding boat. It came out of the water and slid sideways like a hovercraft over the slick sand. When the boat ran out of wet sand, its momentum carried it over the dry sand until it hacked Boy-Face down. Instructor Stoneclam, other instructors, and the ambulance rushed to the wounded man.

Doc started first aid. I never heard Boy-Face call out in pain, but the boat broke both his legs at the thighbones.

When the day finished, most of us hit the showers, but Priest, the punker trainee with Billy Idol hair, grabbed his surfboard and headed out for more. "Those waves are thrashin'!"

CHAPTER 10

Drownproofing

MOST OF THE MEN IN my BUD/S class were about twenty-one years old—I was only nineteen. Together we were a smorgasbord of life: Egyptian army officer, MIT graduate, surfer punk, among others. Each of us had a different reason for becoming a Navy SEAL: to show patriotism, to become king of the surfers, and more. But on a cool winter's morning during training, we all had one thing in common: dread.

The sun was buried in the horizon as my class marched double time through the Naval Amphibious Base in Coronado, California. Today was drownproofing day. I'd always thought drowning was one of the worst ways to die.

Wearing matching camouflage uniforms, we sang out in unison, *looking* confident, but the song of our voices was hollow:

Wake up, wake up, NAB.
We've been up since half past three.

Runnin', swimmin' all day long.
That's what makes a tadpole strong.
Hooyah hey, runnin' day.
Hooyah hey, easy day.

Our anxieties manifested themselves as lingering mists from our warm breath hitting the winter air. The noise of our combat boots struck the black asphalt with melancholy.

When we arrived at the pool located at building 164, we stripped down to our UDT swim shorts. The SEAL instructors watched us with shark eyes as we grouped ourselves in pairs.

"Do you want to go first, or should I?" my partner asked.

"I want to get this over with," I said.

We stood at the deep end of the pool. Goose bumps pricked my flesh as he tied my feet together with high-strength cord.

"Tie it good," I said. "I don't want to have to do this twice."

After finishing the knot, he proceeded to tie my hands behind my back.

I kept my eyes on Stoneclam. He wore his khaki UDT shorts and a dark-blue T-shirt. The T-shirt had a thin gold border on the sleeves. Two cartoony figures were on the left breast: a frog holding a burning stick of dynamite in its hand, and a seal carrying a knife in its mouth. Written in small gold letters were the words "UDT/SEAL Instructor." Kneeling down on one knee, he touched the water reverently, as if to consecrate it for us. He climbed up to the lifeguard chair and took his position.

"You are all going to love this," he said. "Drownproofing is one of my favorites. Sink or swim, sweet peas."

Half the class stood at the edge of the deep end with our feet tied together and hands tied behind our backs. Our partners stood behind us. The instructors were joking, but it was all a peripheral blur to me.

I can't let them get inside my head. I focused on calming my respiration and heartbeat.

"When I give the command, the bound men will hop into the pool," Instructor Stoneclam said. "You must bob up and down twenty times, float for five minutes, swim to the shallow end of the pool, turn around without touching the bottom, swim back to the deep end, do a forward and backward somersault underwater, and retrieve a face mask from the bottom of the pool.

"If your ropes come undone, you must start over from the beginning. If your ropes come undone a second time, you fail. If you break your ropes, I'll let you pass, but don't try it. I only know of one student who ever broke his ropes. We'll be watching you to make sure you don't cheat."

Standing on the edge of the pool, I should have realized how abnormal all this was. Just doing all that bobbing and swimming and somersaults with my hands and feet *free* would be hard enough. I tried to focus on how peaceful the water was. My breathing and heart rate slowed.

Instructor Stoneclam's dark eyes probed us. "First group, enter the water."

The smooth surface of the water broke as we jumped in. A flurry of thoughts assaulted me: panic, suffocation, drowning.

Block the negative. Be calm. Avoid the negative. The heated pool is warm. Focus on the warmth. Become one with the water.

My classmates and I rose and sank at different heights and depths. Some touched the bottom and were already rising to the surface. A negative thought wrestled with me. *The guys at the top are going to breathe while I'm still down here.* I waited helplessly for my feet to touch the bottom. *Wait for the breath. Slow it down. Control the rhythm.* I imagined soft ballet music. My toes touched the concrete bottom. *Don't shoot out of the water like a missile and draw the attention of the instructors.* I gently pushed off. I wanted air, but I couldn't think about it.

My head cleared the surface. I heard screams and saw splashing on the other side of the pool. I closed my eyes and filled my ears with ballet music. My mouth formed a tight circle, sucking a bite of oxygen straight to my lungs, and then I sank slowly to the bottom.

The instructors can't touch me here. The water is my haven.

Pushing off from the bottom again, I opened my eyes as my classmates and I continued to rise and fall. The big Egyptian officer smiled, looking like a brown, oversized water lily. Priest made a goofy face at me and wiggled his body like some sort of wacky water worm as he rose. I smiled, bobbing in the water wearing my imaginary pink tutu.

On one of my trips to the surface, I looked over at the commotion on the other side of the pool. One of my classmates thrashed the water trying to get to the edge of the pool.

"Help me, I'm drowning! Agh!"

Instructor Stoneclam used the lifesaving pole to push him farther away from the edge. "If you were drowning, you wouldn't be telling me about it."

The frightened guy bit the pole.

I took my sip of air and sank down. When I came back up, the hysteric student was being helped out of the pool. He'd had enough of training.

Next, I floated for five minutes. Then I began to dolphin-kick along the length of the pool. *Keep it slow. Keep the rhythm.* I kicked, then turned my head to breathe, sidestroke-style. Kick and breathe, kick and breathe. I reached the shallow end of the pool and began making a turn to the right. Priest was turning left, aimed for a head-on collision course with me. If either of us touched the bottom of the pool, we'd fail. My nerves began to take over, and I started to lose my rhythm. Priest dove underneath me as we made our turn. Our bodies scraped each other, but neither of us touched the bottom. But instead of my anxiety decreasing, it did the opposite.

I struggled my way back to the deep end. There I bobbed once. I did my forward somersault, but I still hadn't recovered my breathing rhythm after the near collision with Priest. Most of my classmates had already finished their forward and backward somersaults, though nineteen face masks still lay on the bottom of the pool. One by one the masks disappeared as each of my buddies grabbed one with his teeth and rose to the surface, completing the job. Now I was the last one in the pool. I could feel Instructor Stoneclam's eyes on me.

I did the backward somersault, my breathing and movement uncoordinated. The threat of failure attacked me as my chlorine-saturated eyes frantically searched the blurry bottom for a face mask. I spotted one mask at the opposite side of the deep end.

I can't make it that far.

Suddenly, my blurred vision caught sight of another mask down to my left. I sunk down and my feet touched the bottom, my toes only inches away from the mask, and I dropped to my knees. I tried to lean over to grasp it with my teeth. But I had swallowed too much air during my somersaults, and my body floated up before I could bite the mask. My body stopped halfway up. There was no air in my lungs to float me to the top and too much air in my stomach to allow me to sink to the bottom. The taste of chlorine made me want to vomit.

Fear stepped aside to let discouragement make its entrance. And it was infinitely more powerful than fear. I felt myself shrinking. I heard voices—my classmates cheering me on. They seemed so far away. I was too weak. *I've failed.* Discouragement smashed me, destroying every particle of energy inside me. Discouragement raised its hammer high in the air, preparing to make its final blow. But I didn't want it to end this way. I'd come so far.

That's when I got angry. Angry at fear and discouragement for ganging up on me. Angry at Instructor Stoneclam. Angry at anything that would get in my way of succeeding, including myself. My spirit exploded. Its heat and power rumbled through me, the shock wave overwhelming my senses.

I kicked rapidly, propelling myself upward. I surfaced with half my body shooting out of the water. I flipped like an angry fish and dove headfirst back into the water, frantically kicking my tied feet.

I shot down toward the mask, and my forehead smashed into the floor. I twisted my head around and clenched the black strap with my teeth. I kicked and wiggled without oxygen, managing to swim toward the top. I felt so dizzy.

Complete the mission. I struggled halfway to the surface. My body was heavy. My peripheral vision faded. I kicked harder. My body started to tingle. Every part of me craved oxygen as the gray circle around my vision became smaller, darker. I felt like I was losing consciousness; it was *getting harder and harder to focus on anything*.

I managed to poke my head out of the water and suck in some air. Madly, my feet kept kicking. Some classmates started to applaud.

"Shut up!" Instructor Stoneclam barked.

I refused to stop kicking unless Stoneclam told my partner to help me out, and I refused to let go of the mask. Instructor Stoneclam studied me leisurely. I sucked air and water in through my teeth. I figured he could let my buddy help me out from the pool, or when I became unconscious and sank to the bottom, Stoneclam could rescue me himself. Either way, I wasn't going to let go of the mask.

"Pull him out," Instructor Stoneclam told my partner.

Incredible relief coursed through me as he and another student pulled me out. The ground felt strange, and I had to sit down because my legs weren't supporting me well. My classmates untied my hands. I felt like a fish, not knowing what to do with my free extremities except flap the kinks out of my wrists. My head ached, and steam rolled off my wet body.

"I've never seen anyone pull their mask out like that," one of the instructors told me. "You'll have to teach us your technique."

The other instructors smiled. But Instructor Stoneclam just barked, "Next!"

I got as good a grip on my limbs as I could and helped tie my partner's feet and hands.

"Second group, enter the water," Instructor Stoneclam said.

As my partner made a splash, I no longer thought drowning was one of the worst ways to die. Drownproofing replaced my old fear with a new one: failing without trying everything I could to catch my dreams.

CHAPTER 11

Phase One

D URING THE THREE WEEKS OF Indoc, we went through a lot. One day we earned our face masks by swimming, performing calisthenics, and singing "America the Beautiful" while wearing face masks full of water. It was a garbled aberration, and that evening while eating dinner in the cafeteria, my eyes were so saturated with chlorine that the whole world looked foggy.

On another day, we swam in the pool with fins, and my swim ranking improved from second-to-last in the class to the upper half of my class. We had to swim one thousand yards with fins in twenty minutes or less. Those who failed were dropped. Each activity was doable, but the requirements kept coming and coming and standards rose and rose in what seemed like an eternal hike.

I just have to keep believing I can make it.

Indoc ended and Phase One of BUD/S training began with a new cadre of hardcore SEAL instructors. While we sat in a classroom, the instructors introduced themselves and yelled at some of us for nodding off. The instructors made us do push-ups until our arms became soggy. We could see the shit storm on the horizon.

The only easy day was yesterday.

All we had to do to quit was walk outside to a pole where a ship's bell was attached, place our helmet liner on the concrete, and ring the bell three times. As soon as the Phase One instructors finished giving their self-introductions, a number of my classmates left the room quietly, and the bell rang repeatedly.

One chilly day, we earned our wetsuits with a swim in San Diego Bay. The wind chopped the water, making the swim more challenging and the air colder. We swam fast to stay warm, but some guys slowed down and seemed to feel sorry for themselves, keeping them in the water longer and making them colder. Hands popped up across the bay for early extractions—they wanted to ring the bell. I couldn't understand why. Sure, it was cold, but I didn't think it was cold enough to quit.

Each week, the standards were raised. We had to run four miles on the beach in thirty-two minutes or less, swim two miles in the open ocean in ninety-five minutes or less, and complete the obstacle course in seventeen minutes or under.

As the third week of Phase One neared an end, Lieutenant Morris, the Phase One officer, called many of my classmates into his office individually. The instructors were thinking about firing some students before the fourth week—Hell Week. Wearing my inspection uniform and shined boots, I waited outside the door when it was my turn. I felt isolated, and suddenly I didn't have control of my own destiny. *This could be the end.* Most of the blood flushed from my face, and weakness overcame me.

Instructor Benelli led me into the office. With my helmet under my arm, I stood at attention in front of a large table where Lieutenant Morris, Doc, and some other instructors sat.

"Stephen Templin, reporting as ordered, sir."

"Do you know why you're in this room right now?" Lieutenant Morris said.

"No, sir, I don't."

He said nothing.

A lot of BUD/S was a big mind game. Instructors probed for weaknesses like sharks circling the water, and when they found one, they attacked. They sometimes even created a perception that a student had a weakness until the student believed it actually existed. My greatest weakness had been swimming without fins, but now we swam with fins. At nineteen years old, I was less mature than the older guys, but if that was an issue for kicking me out, someone should've told me. Rather than chase the endless tails of BUD/S games, I knew it was time to defend my strengths, however few there were. It was time to defend my right to stay in the game.

"I keep up with the PT. My run times are good. My swim times with fins have been at the top half of my class. I hold the record in the obstacle course. I thought I was doing well in Phase One, sir."

"This is one of the best classes I have taught. I think that after my instructors and I fire a no-load or two, this class has a chance to complete Hell Week with no one quitting."

My pulse pounded, and my mouth went dry.

His eyes burned into mine. "Are you going to quit during Hell Week?"

"No, sir," I said.

"Don't disappoint me."

That day, I got to stay, but they did fire one of my classmates. It was their prerogative. If they didn't want a guy serving with them in the teams, they were out. I just had to make sure it didn't happen to me.

CHAPTER 12

From Circus to Medal of Honor

In BUD/S training, those of us who couldn't keep up on a run were gathered up for the greatest show on earth—the circus of pain. The circus performers had to jump into the ocean, then roll along the beach, saltwater helping the sand cling to every orifice and crack of the body, rubbing like sandpaper. Each circus performer did calisthenics until every major muscle, and some minor muscles they didn't know they had, ached. Some guys left the circus by ringing out. Some tried harder and successfully made sure they weren't rounded up into the circus again. But others, even though they gave more than 110 percent, found themselves in the circus after every run, because even their bests weren't good enough.

I think a lot of guys would agree with me when I say that I have the greatest respect for the circus performers who worked harder than everyone else and somehow managed to scrape by. More than the gazelles running ahead, more than the fish in front, more than the O-Course monkeys, these underdogs were the toughest. One of the most famous of these circus performers was Thomas Norris.

Norris had wanted to join the FBI, but Uncle Sam drafted him instead. So he joined the navy to become a pilot. But his eyesight quickly disqualified him. So he volunteered for BUD/S, where he often fell to the rear on runs and swims. There was often talk among instructors about firing him, but Norris didn't give up. He became a SEAL. And boy, did he make a comeback . . .

In 1972 in Vietnam, two pilots of a surveillance aircraft went down deep in enemy territory where over thirty thousand North Vietnamese Army (NVA) prepared for an Easter offensive. In the most expensive rescue attempt of the Vietnam War, fourteen men were killed, eight aircraft downed, two rescuers captured, and two more rescuers stranded in enemy territory. As an air rescue became impossible, they needed another tactic and quick. So Lieutenant Norris led a five-man Vietnamese SEAL patrol into the area, located one of the pilots, and returned him to the Forward Operating Base (FOB). The NVA retaliated with a rocket attack on the FOB, killing two of the Vietnamese SEALs, among others.

Norris and his three remaining Vietnamese SEALs failed once to rescue the second pilot. Because of the impossibility of the situation, two of the remaining three weren't willing to risk their lives for another rescue attempt. So Norris and the Vietnamese SEAL Nguyen Van Kiet made another attempt—and failed a second time.

But on April 12, about ten days after the plane had been shot down, Norris got a report of the pilot's location. He and Kiet disguised themselves as fishermen and paddled their sampan upriver into the foggy night. They located the pilot at dawn on the riverbank, hidden under vegetation. They helped him into their sampan and covered him with bamboo and banana leaves. A group of enemy on land spotted them but couldn't get through the thick jungle as fast as Norris and Kiet could paddle on the water. When they approached the FOB, an NVA patrol spotted the rescuers and poured heavy machine-gun fire down on them. Norris called in an air strike to keep the enemies' heads down and a smoke screen to blind them. Norris and Kiet took the pilot into the FOB, where Norris gave him first aid until he was evacuated. Lieutenant Norris received the Medal of Honor for his part in the rescue, and Kiet received the Navy Cross, the highest award given to a foreign national.

About six months later, Norris faced the jaws of adversity yet again. Lieutenant Norris chose Petty Officer Michael Thornton for a mission, who then selected two Vietnamese SEALs to aid him, Dang and Quan. One shaky Vietnamese officer named Tai was also assigned to the team. Carrying AK-47s and lots of ammo, they rode a South Vietnamese Navy junk (US Navy ships were unavailable) up the South China Sea, planning to launch a rubber boat from the junk and then patrol on land to gather intelligence. The junk had inserted them too far north, however, so Norris walked the point with Thornton on rear security and the Vietnamese SEALs between them. They soon realized they were in North Vietnam. While hiding in their day layup position, Tai, without consulting Norris or Thornton, ordered the two Vietnamese SEALs to do a poorly designed prisoner snatch on a nearby two-man patrol. Dang and Quan came up empty-handed and, in the process, alerted the two-man patrol to their presence.

Thornton knocked out one of the enemies with his rifle butt, so he couldn't contact the nearby village, but the other enemy escaped, only to return with between fifty and seventy-five NVA regulars. In the meantime, the SEALs bound the knocked-out enemy, then, when he became conscious, interrogated him.

Norris and Dang shot at the NVA regulars, and Norris radioed for naval gunfire support, providing their coordinates, positions, and the types of rounds needed. The navy operator on the other end was unfamiliar with fire support for ground troops. While trying to talk him through it, Norris had to put down the phone for a moment to shoot. When he got back on the radio, his call had been transferred to another ship, but they were under enemy fire and unable to help. Norris and his men were on their own.

Norris and Dang moved back while shooting at the enemy, and Thornton put the Vietnamese lieutenant on the rear while he and Quan defended the flanks. Thornton shot several NVA, took cover, rose in a different position, and shot again. Although the enemy popped up from the same spot each time, they didn't know where Thornton was or how many people were with him. While maneuvering to the rear, he aimed at a far sand dune and squeezed the trigger. One of the NVA hiding on the other side screamed.

After about five hours of fighting, Norris finally made radio contact with a ship that could help—the *Newport News*. But before help arrived, the enemy threw a Chinese communist (Chicom) grenade in Thornton's direction. He threw it back. The enemy threw it again. Thornton threw it back. When the grenade came back a third time, Thornton dove for cover. The grenade exploded, six pieces of shrapnel striking Thornton's back.

"Mike, buddy," Norris called. "Mike, buddy!" But Thornton stayed quiet. About four enemy soldiers ran over to Thornton's position. He shot all four. Two fell on top of him and the other two fell backward.

"I'm all right!" Thornton called. "It's just shrapnel."

Then the enemy went silent.

The SEALs began to leapfrog. Norris laid down cover fire so Thornton, Quan, and Tai could retreat. Then Thornton and Dang would do the same while Norris and his team moved back. Norris brought up a LAW rocket to shoot when an NVA with an AK-47 came out of nowhere and shot him in the face, knocking him off a sand dune. Norris tried to get up to return fire but passed out.

As Dang ran back to Thornton, two rounds hit the radio Dang carried on his back.

"Where's Tommy?" Thornton asked.

"He dead."

"Are you sure?"

Dang looked down. "He shot in face."

"Are you sure?"

"I saw it."

Thornton was fired up. "Stay here. I'll go back and get him."

"No, Mike. He dead. Enemy coming."

"Y'all stay here."

Thornton ran about five hundred yards to Norris's position through a hail of enemy fire. He killed several NVA in order to get next to Norris's body. The bullet had entered the side of Norris's head and blown out the front of his forehead. Even Thornton thought his buddy was dead. He threw Norris's body over his shoulder in a fireman's carry and grabbed Norris's AK. Thornton had already used up eight grenades and his LAW rockets and was down to one or two magazines of ammo.

Suddenly, the first round from the *Newport News* came in like a Volkswagen flying through the air. When it exploded, it threw Thornton down a twenty- or thirty-foot dune. Norris's body flew high over Thornton's head. Thornton hurried over to Norris.

"Tommy, buddy," Thornton said.

Norris moved.

Thornton smiled. "The SOB's alive."

Thornton picked him up, put him on his shoulders, and took off running as Dang and Quan gave cover fire.

The navy artillery round had bought them some time, but now that time had expired. Enemy rounds came at the SEALs again.

Thornton reached Dang and Quan's position. "Where's Tai?"

One of the Vietnamese explained that when Thornton went back to get Norris, Tai had abandoned them, running into the water.

"When I yell 'one,' Quan, I want you to lay down a base of fire," Thornton said, moving on without Tai. "When I yell 'two,' Dang, you lay down a base of fire. And on 'three,' I'll lay down a base of fire. And we'll leapfrog back to the water."

But as they got to the water's edge, Thornton fell. He didn't know it at the time, but he'd been shot through his left calf. He picked up Norris and carried him under his arm the rest of the way. Then he felt a floundering movement, quickly learning that he had unwittingly pushed Norris's head under the water. Thornton got his buddy's head above water and searched for Norris's life vest. Per standard operating procedure (SOP) for Team Two SEALs, his vest was tied to his leg, making it difficult to access now that they were in the water, so Thornton put his vest on Norris, using it to keep them both afloat.

Quan fluttered in the water, the right side of his hip shot off. Thornton grabbed him, and Quan hung on to Norris and their one life preserver. Kicking out to sea, Thornton could see bullets traveling through the water.

"Do we got everybody?" Norris asked, barely conscious. He could see Quan and Dang but not the officer. Pushing down on Thornton to get a better view, he saw Tai, far out to sea, before he blacked out again.

After swimming well out of the enemy's range of fire, Thornton, Dang, and Quan watched as the *Newport News* left the area. With bodies scattered over the ground, the ship's crew must've thought the SEALs were dead.

"What do we do, now?" one of the SEALs asked.

"Swim south," Thornton said. He put two four-by-four battle dresses on Norris's head, but they couldn't cover the entire wound. And Norris was going into shock.

Meanwhile, unknown to Thornton at the time, some of his SEAL teammates were searching for them in a junk. They found Tai and debriefed him before finding Norris, Thornton, Dang, and Quan. Thornton radioed the *Newport News* for pickup.

On board the *Newport News,* Thornton carried Norris to medical. The medical team cleaned up Norris as best they could. "He's never going to make it," the doctor said.

But Norris was medevaced to Da Nang regardless. From there, they flew him to the Philippines, where he proved the doctor wrong. He was transferred to the Naval Medical Center in Bethesda, Maryland. After years of major surgeries, he'd permanently lost part of his skull and his eye.

For Thornton's actions, he received the Medal of Honor.

The navy retired Norris, but he still says the only easy day was yesterday. Norris returned to his childhood dream of becoming an FBI agent, and in 1979, he requested a disability waiver.

"If you can pass the same test as anybody else applying for this organization," FBI director William Webster said, "I will waiver your disabilities." Of course, Norris passed.

In the FBI, Norris tried to become a member of the newly forming Hostage Rescue Team (HRT). But the FBI's bean counters and pencil pushers didn't want to allow a one-eyed man on the team. HRT founder Danny Coulson overruled them, though.

"We'll probably have to take another Congressional Medal of Honor winner with one eye if he applies," he said, "but I'll take the risk."

After twenty years with the FBI, many of them as an assault team leader, Norris retired. He'd sure come a long way since the circus at BUD/S.

CHAPTER 13

Between a Rock and a Hard Place

Hell Week had begun. We still hadn't returned the bell to the SEAL instructors, but that was only round one. Round two started now.

They'd ordered us to paddle our boats north, through the night to Hotel del Coronado. It was a resort hotel, but we wouldn't be checking in. Stopping outside the surf zone, where the waves couldn't thrash us, we looked to shore for our signal. There an instructor flashed the green light signal. The first boat crew went in, followed by the others. Then it was my crew's turn.

We caught a good wave and paddled hard to ride it all the way in. As we neared the big black boulders, it seemed like waves were hitting us from three different directions. Our speed kept the water from knocking us around and capsizing us, but we slammed into the boulders, and *hard*. Bodies flew out of the boat like Pop-Tarts from a toaster.

Even though the instructors had taught us to never get between the boat and the rocks, that was right where Martinez and I ended up. Our boat stood nearly straight up, the stern jammed down between two boulders, water partly filling it. Martinez and I tried to push it off us while the others pulled from the opposite side. It was like trying to move a dead whale.

The next wave came in so mightily that it knocked the rest of my crew off their feet, smashing them onto the rocks. That wave pressed the dead whale with so much force that Martinez and I didn't have enough arm strength to push it off our chests. My back cracked. One of our guys fell into the ocean. The others who could regain their footing on the slippery boulders helped pull him out.

Another wave came. I didn't even try to resist. It pressed the boat against my chest so hard that I knew my chest would pop.

As the wave receded, our boat leader shouted, "Pull!"

Martinez and I tried again to push the boat off us while our classmates on the other side pulled. Then another wave came. Instead of fighting the ocean, my classmates braced for the crash. This time it squeezed the breath out of my lungs, and I could feel my rib cage bend to the edge of nearly snapping.

So this is how I die.

Maybe it sounds strange, but I felt surprisingly calm about it.

After the wave swept back out to sea, my classmates were still on their feet, and they pulled on the boat like madmen.

Martinez and I shoved with everything we had and then some. Finally, we freed the boat from the rocks. I was so relieved to be alive that I'd forgotten all about being cold.

We carried our boat onto the beach, and an instructor greeted us. "Are you enjoying your vacation?"

"Hooyah!"

"Drop!" he said.

We did push-ups 'til our arms seemed like they would fall off.

A young couple from the nearby hotel had been on the beach for an early-morning stroll when they came over to view the festivities. The woman wore a neon-orange sweater, and tears streamed down her face. It struck me as ironic. We were the ones who should've been crying.

We did more push-ups until the last boat crew came in. A third of their boat hung deflated, shredded by the rocks. They thought they were finished, but an instructor sent them back out in the ocean again. The next time, they came back with only about a third of the boat. This time, when the crew started to go back out again, the instructor stopped them.

The instructors didn't even try to fight us for the bell this time. But the game was far from over . . .

CHAPTER 14

The Little Match Girl

It was a Monday evening, and we assembled, cold and shivering, on Turner Field at the NAB. Like the poor Little Match Girl from the fable, sitting in the snow watching the flame from her match burn down the stick, we watched the sun fall from the sky. The Little Match Girl knew her father would beat her if she returned home without having sold the matches. In contrast, we were going to get punished no matter what we did.

We'd been without sleep for nearly twenty-four hours, and the real world was beginning to blend into the dream world. Like when a group of instructors—that would later be known as the Evil Trio—replaced our current SEAL instructors and stood in front of the headlights of a parked truck. The appearance of the Evil Trio was no dream.

Instructor Blah led the Evil Trio. "Good-bye, sun," he spoke in a monotone into his megaphone. "Good-bye, sun. Good-bye, sun."

The sun disappeared then, taking its warmth and our hopes with it.

"Maybe we should just give it to them," said Priest.
"Come on, man. Don't quit now," we reasoned with him.
"But I can't take this anymore," Priest said.
"Just stay a little longer."

Priest walked toward the Evil Trio. Someone grabbed ahold of his arm, stopping him.

"Let me go," he said.
"Don't go," some of us pleaded.

There was a struggle, and another classmate assisted in holding Priest back. Someone else said we shouldn't physically restrain him. An argument broke out among us, and Priest wrestled himself free and ran to the instructors.

Ensign Mark and another followed Priest partway and tried to persuade him to return with us, but he only ran faster to the instructors. Even so, there was no bell for him to ring out with.

The instructors spoke with Priest, but they were too far away for us to hear their words. "Okay, guys. Priest wants to quit. It's time to bring back the bell."

Murmuring broke out among us, but we didn't give in.

"Come on guys, give us the bell," Instructor Blah said.

No dice.

"Mr. Mark, can we have a word with you?"

Ensign Mark walked away from us and joined the instructors. The Evil Trio, Mark, and Priest talked. Then Mark returned to us. "Priest really does want to quit," he said. "We have to give back the bell."

As a class, we agreed to give it back, and the instructors drove the man who knew where the bell was hidden back to the barracks.

We waited at Turner Field for about half an hour until the instructors returned with our guy and the bell, which he'd stowed in the trunk of his car. Priest rang it more than the requisite three times. We were in a field, but it was as if we were in a burning building with the fire alarm ringing and guys running for the nearest exit. We tried to encourage them to stay, but they weren't open to discussing it. The bell kept ringing as more guys Dropped on Request (DOR).

When the bell stopped ringing, we were told to report our status to the boat crew leaders, who held a powwow. Next, we reorganized our boat crews and loaded a black rubber boat onto the back of the instructors' truck. We'd lost seven classmates total, enough to man a whole boat.

Instructor Blah gathered us around him and explained our next task: Lyon's Lope. Named after Vietnam veteran SEAL Ted Lyon, Lyon's Lope was a torturous boat Olympics. First we raced on land without boats, and then we ran with the boats balanced on our heads. Next, we rowed our boats out into San Diego Bay, flipped them over in the frigid water, and righted them before racing back to shore. Finally, without the boats, each crew had to form a human centipede in the bay. Each man wrapped his legs around the man in front of him, and then we all used our arms for paddles to race the other crews. My crew was losing, and we shivered violently, the cold numbing our brains so much that we scarcely knew who we were or what we were doing. The longer we stayed in the water, the dumber we became, and the dumber we became, the longer we stayed in the water. Finally, we finished the race and crawled onto land.

Our crew members had second-degree hypothermia after that, and Doc inspected each of us to make sure we hadn't slipped into third-degree hypothermia, which would've been critical.

"What's your name?" he asked me.

"Templin," I said.

"Where are you?" Doc asked.

"Turner Field."

"How many fingers am I holding up?"

"Three," I said.

"Nope, try again."

"Three."

"Nope."

I stared at him hopelessly. I could only say what I saw.

"I'm just screwing with you," Doc said.

My whole class stood on shore. We stared blankly at each other like a platoon of zombies.

"Well, Lyon's Lope was fun," Instructor Blah said in his megaphone. "It was so much fun, we're going to do it again."

I didn't know how I could possibly do it again, but for me, quitting wasn't an option. For others, it was, and they rang the bell right then and there. The Evil Trio had lived up to their reputation by retrieving the bell and taking the first chunks out of our ranks—in a big way—but they didn't actually make us do Lyon's Lope again. The instructors acted like they wanted everyone to quit, but really, they only wanted the quitters to quit.

CHAPTER 15

Monday Midrats

At midnight, we departed the cold darkness outside to enter the bright warmth of the Naval Amphibious Base cafeteria. With the flick of a mental switch, I turned off Hell Week. *Forget about what happened, and forget about what will happen. Savor the cafeteria, now—these moments are too few and far between to waste.*

Our SEAL instructors had told us that most guys lose weight during Hell Week, so I focused on making sure that didn't happen to me. I got in the chow line and loaded my plate. From behind the counter, a cute Filipina with almond-shaped eyes and a warm smile served my plate of hot food. Seeing her made me feel alive, and I thought she was real, but like a Hell Week hallucination, I'd never see her again—except in my memories.

My mother was a good cook, but I thought navy food was excellent: chicken adobo from the Philippines, *yakisoba* from Japan, steak, lobster . . . During Hell Week we were given four meals a day. We called the midnight meal "midrats," short for "midnight rations." Rather than prepare a separate meal, the cooks would heat up leftovers from the evening meal. But even the navy's leftovers are better than a lot of meals I've eaten.

Some guys would drink coffee with their meals, but I was never a coffee drinker. Steam rose from my hot water, and I was too tired to mess around with a packet of cocoa. The warm mug thawed my numb hands as a sandy puddle of seawater formed around my feet. Piss and sweat—we smelled like swamp monsters. (The Hell Week pace was so busy that most of us only had time to piss ourselves, which also served as a moment of warm relief from the cold.)

While we ate, some guys talked, and others stayed quiet. I couldn't understand how the talkers had the energy to jack their jaws like that, but it was probably better to expend the energy talking to others than feeling sorry for oneself in solitude. I was one of the quiet ones, focused on enjoying the moment—peace, light, warmth. Some guys ate like wolves, and others nibbled like rabbits. I was one of the wolves. The rabbits would suffer later when their fuel tanks hit empty.

I looked around the cafeteria as I chowed. A group of SEAL instructors ate at a separate table. They wouldn't harass us unless one of us fell asleep before our thirty-minute meal was over.

We finished up and got ready to head back out into the cold, black, cruel world. With another flick of my mental switch, I turned the cafeteria off and Hell Week back on. Once outside, before the tortures even resumed, the bell rang, and we lost another guy. I was too zoned into my own little Hell Week world to think about him or his reasons why.

CHAPTER 16

It Pays to Be a Winner

THE NEXT DAY, WE DID Run-Paddle-Run, racing along the beach carrying the IBSs on our heads. The black rubber boats banged against the tops of our skulls as we ran, and our feet pounded the ground below, the two forces seeming to impact at our knees, making it harder than it already was to run. And we short-legged crews ate the sand of the long-legged crews as they sped ahead.

Of course, my crew paid for losing in the form of IBS push-ups—holding our boat over our heads and pushing it up and down—until we reached exhaustion. Then we dropped the boat and did push-ups with our legs propped up on the sides, which put extra gravity on our arms while the instructors shoveled sand on us, covering us with it. Faces in the beach, having spent almost all the strength in our upper bodies, we wiggled until we got our heads off the ground and could prop ourselves up on our arms. Then almost every one of us collapsed at the elbows, dumping our faces in the sand, again. Wiggle, prop, collapse. Wiggle, prop, collapse. Those were our push-ups.

But where we had failed on land, we made up for in the water, coming in first place. I don't know if it was because we had more upper-body strength, better technique, or smaller bodies to transport, but my crew cruised in the ocean. After we crossed the finish line, we got to catch a breather while the losers took their turn with the IBS push-ups and sand-eating drills. It was about time.

CHAPTER 17

Cold Steel

DAYS AND NIGHTS BLENDED INTO one constant blur. One legendary Hell Week event took place on a steel pier where the navy docks its small boats. The instructors told us to take off our jungle-combat boots. My fingers were so numb and shaky from the cold that I had a tough time untying the laces, but I managed to get out of my boots and placed them upright on the pier. Then we were instructed to remove our socks and belts and stuff them in our boots.

The steel pier felt like ice under my bare feet. I started telling myself, *The water is warm here. It's like a hot tub.* I kept repeating it to myself and imagining how warm it was, but the mind trick wasn't really working.

Still wearing our muted-green uniforms, we jumped into the bay with no life jackets, shoes, or socks. I immediately executed a dead man's float while I undid the fly on my trousers. The Velcro saved my numb fingers from having to fumble with a tiny zipper. Of course, this wasn't navy-issue Velcro. Before

Hell Week, one of our ensigns, some classmates, and I had taken our trousers to a tailor in San Diego where most of the students went for uniform needs. In preparation for Hell Week, we asked the tailor to replace our zippers with Velcro, knowing enough about what was in store to know it would help.

Still doing a dead man's float, I brought my face out of the freezing water and took a quick bite of oxygen, then resumed my position facedown in the water. When I started to sink too much, I kicked a couple of strokes. Meanwhile, I pulled off my trousers, then Velcroed the fly shut. With my trousers now off, I tied a square knot at the end of each leg. Then, using both hands, I grabbed hold of the waist and kicked until my body straightened up from its float. I lifted my pants high in the air, then slammed them forward and down on the water, trapping air in the trouser legs.

As my upper body hung over the valley in the V of my homemade trouser-flotation device, I became a bit tranquil. I had been so concerned about drowning that I had forgotten how frigid the water was. Now that I had things under control, though, the cold crept back in. I tried to imagine steam rising around me in my hot tub.

Some of the guys swam back to the pier. We tried to convince them not to, but they'd had enough. *Ring, ring, ring.*

"If one more of you rings the bell, the rest of you can come out of the water, too," Senior Chief said. "Inside the ambulance we have warm blankets and a thermos of hot coffee."

Someone began singing. "Now Superman was the man of steel!"

It picked up our spirits, and we joined in.

Now Superman was a man of steel,
But he ain't no match for a Navy SEAL.
Now Chief and Supe, they got in a fight.
Chief hit him in the head with some kryptonite.
Supe fell to his knees in pain—
Now Chief's dating Lois Lane.
Now Chief and Batman had one, too.
Chief hit him in the head with his shoe.
Hit him in the temple with his left heel.
Now Chief's driving the Batmobile.

"If you can sing that with my name instead of 'Chief,'" Senior Chief said, "I'll let you out of the water!"

We sang the tune again with his name in place of "Chief." The revised version with Senior Chief's name added too many syllables, destroying the song's rhythm, but Senior liked it. "Everybody out of the water!" he said.

"Hooyah!"

We crawled out of the water and onto the floating steel pier.

"Now strip down to your undershorts and lie down on the pier. If you don't have shorts, your birthday suit is even better."

I stripped down to my black triathlon shorts and lay down. The triathlon shorts were my choice because they dried faster than a fabric like cotton, didn't chafe the skin, and gave more support and protection than being naked. The instructors had prepared the pier by spraying it down with water. Mother Nature had prepared the pier by blowing cool wind across it. It was like lying down on a wet block of ice. Then the instructors sprayed *us* with cold water. My muscles contracted wildly, the spasms uncontrollable. We all flapped around on the steel deck like fish out of water.

Our leading petty officer started singing, and we jumped right in, looking for any kind of distraction.

> I had a dog whose name was Blue.
> He wanted to be a SEAL, too!
> So I bought him a mask and four tiny little fins,
> Took him to the ocean and threw him in.
> Blue came back, to my surprise,
> With a shark in his teeth and a gleam in his eyes!

Our singing kept us together and successfully kept our minds off the stinging cold. We didn't lose any more guys at the steel pier that night.

CHAPTER 18

Sandman

WE HADN'T SLEPT SINCE WE woke up Sunday at midnight. Then on what I think was Wednesday morning, we were ordered to the barracks to sleep. I crashed on top of my bed with my clothes and boots on. As soon as my head hit the pillow, I skipped the shallow stages of sleep and hit instant deep sleep.

I was one of the lucky ones in that regard. Some guys weren't able to sleep at all. It made sense: when that jacked up, it could understandably become almost impossible to shut everything down. Others apparently *chose* not to sleep, something I'd never understood. Sleep can help a person think straight. Though, I was told we only slept about an hour and a half. I felt like I'd slept a lot longer, and I exaggerated that in my mind to make it feel like I'd slept even longer. I felt like a new man—battered, but new.

CHAPTER 19

The Great Race

WEDNESDAY AFTERNOON, WE TOOK OFF on a land race, carrying our boats across two miles of beach north of the BUD/S training facility. Then we raced the two miles back to the facility. Consistent with my boat crew's land racing, we came in dead last. While my losing boat crew performed all manner of acrobatics for the instructors on the beach, the other boat crews were already in the Pacific Ocean paddling south.

Lieutenant Morris's eyes burned into us while we grunted and groaned under the IBS. "I will be waiting for you at the end of this next race. I will be displeased if this boat crew comes in last. Am I clear?"

"Hooyah!" we said.

"Do not disappoint me."

My crew hit the water like men possessed. I stretched forward and drove my paddle deep into the ocean, then pulled back as far as I could while keeping it fully submerged. Then I pulled the oar out to repeat the process. I pushed all the power in my shoulders into the movement. The smaller muscles in my arms and hands focused on balance and support—using them as the main power source would only burn me out. I breathed long, deep breaths through the circle I'd created with my lips, directing the air straight to my lungs. Our paddles pumped in and out of the water with the rhythm of an internal combustion engine.

It wasn't long before we passed one of the other boats, moving us out of last place. My crew continued to dig deep and long as we passed more boats. I really thought we had stroked all the way to Mexico, but we were still in the United States. We had paddled about six miles at nonstop turbo speed to the Silver Strand State Beach. We closed in on the boat in the lead, Ensign Mark's.

I could see the instructors standing around a portable beach marker on the shore, the site for our insertion. Ensign Mark and his crew neared the location in the water where they'd need to turn left and paddle toward the beach.

"Cut them off!" our boat leader yelled. "Go for the beach marker now!"

We headed for shore early, gliding along the water at an angle. If the waves had been high, the move would have been unthinkable, wiping us out, but our turbo paddling kept the small waves from tipping us over sideways.

Ensign Mark's crew paddled crazy fast, like cartoon characters, in response. They landed just south of the marker, overshooting it. We landed north of it, undershooting. Both of our crews sprinted with our boats to the insertion point, dropped the boats, and scrambled to prepare for inspection as our boat leaders reported to the instructors.

"Smurf Crew," one instructor called, "you are the winners! Take a seat!"

We couldn't contain our joy. "Hooyah!"

"Ensign Mark's boat crew," he said, "up boat."

Mark's crew raised their boat to the typical extended-arm carry position.

"Smurf Crew started in the water last, but they beat you! Why?"

Mark's crew moaned and groaned under the weight of their boat. "They cheated, Instructor," Ensign Mark said. "They cut us off at an angle."

The instructor laughed. "Push 'em out."

My crew watched Mark's crew do overhead push-ups with their IBS while we sat in our boat bathing in sunbeams. Being warm and dry felt like heaven.

Lieutenant Morris walked up to us. "It pays to be a winner, doesn't it, Smurf Crew?"

"Hooyah!"

We called our location Camp Surf. When the other crews arrived, they worked off their losers' debt, just as Mark's had. Then our class hobbled around a wide sandy beach looking for firewood. I wandered around in circles like a zombie. An empty-handed zombie. That is, until Senior Chief injected me with a bit of a morale booster in the form of push-ups. Even when gathering firewood, it pays to be a winner.

CHAPTER 20

Chicken à la Sand

My class was divided into two groups. Using only our hands, each group dug a large pit in the Camp Surf sand. When the two pits were big enough, we sat in them. Then the instructors tossed us boxed meals. As we started to eat, the instructors shoveled sand on us. I shielded my food with my body and ate as fast as I could, but my main course quickly became chicken à la sand.

After wolfing that down, I only had time to eat the crackers sprinkled with beach debris, pocketing the peanut butter packet for later. I'd been hoping to have some dessert, but just as I pulled out my cookie, an instructor side-slung a shovelful of sand directly at me. Ignoring the grit in my eyes, I spit the stuff out of my mouth, blew on my cookie, and brushed the sand off with my hand. Tasted a bit gravelly, but a full meal topped off with a cookie boosted my morale and replenished my fuel. I put a packet of ground pepper in my pocket, leaving nothing to waste.

The whole meal took me about five minutes. A number of my classmates, however, had just sat there with cardboard boxes full of food and sand, moronic looks on their faces, and empty stomachs.

After our meal, the sun went down and the tide came in. We dug frantically, building up the walls of our pit to keep the water out. The instructors ordered us to stop building and sit down. Little by little the seawater started seeping into the other group's pit. They hadn't built their walls high enough. The instructors ordered us to our feet and to switch pits. We sat down in our classmates' soggy-bottomed pit while they sat dry in ours. But the other group didn't stay dry long—seawater soon broke through the walls. The instructors wouldn't let us get out until we had a refreshingly long bath, Hell Week–style.

CHAPTER 21

Good Cop, Bad Cop

LATER THAT NIGHT, AN INSTRUCTOR gathered us near a bonfire. He was a black SEAL, but in the teams, everyone was the same shade of green. "I'm proud of you guys. If you made it to Wednesday night of Hell Week, you'll make it all the way."

Some of my classmates gathered around the SEAL instructor as he joked and told stories about his life in the teams, smiling and laughing with one another, while others of us gathered around the fire. Martinez and I looked at each other skeptically. It seemed we were the only ones who believed the SEAL instructor wasn't suddenly our new friend—he was still the enemy. Martinez and I stayed close to the fire, enjoying the warmth even as our wet clothing smoldered. We could see the instructor, but he was difficult to hear from where we stood. The whole time, I couldn't stop thinking, *I want to get in the ocean. The ocean is so warm and peaceful. I want to get in the ocean. I want to get in the ocean.*

I looked around at my fellow trainees and saw Petty Officer Lin standing away from the fire, shivering. Lin had been halfway through Hell Week once before when he'd been pulled for hypothermia. I wasn't sure why he didn't come over to warm up, but my guess was that he figured his body would experience less shock going from cold to colder ocean water once we were back to our drills. I had the opposite idea, though, and hoped it would take my body temperature longer to drop from fire hot to cold ocean water.

"You guys are catching on fire," one of my classmates said to Martinez and me.

"Thanks," I said, but we remained in place, determined to keep up our new tactic. When my front got too hot to withstand, I turned around to heat up my back. I popped open my packet of peanut butter and spread it on the cracker I'd also saved. I ate it slowly, savoring it as I continued to keep my mind on getting back in the water.

The joking and stories went on until Instructor Benelli arrived to relieve the other instructor. I was glad he was the one who'd be leading us in our next drill. Actually, we all liked the Italian Stallion, as we called him. Even when he'd given me and two other guys some extra attention for our Italian heritage, he kept us smiling. On weekends, with his leather jacket, thick black mustache, and Harley-Davidson motorcycle, he looked like a Hell's Angel, and his booming laughter was infectious.

We were excited to see him and made it clear. "Hooyah, Instructor Benelli!"

"What are you people doing?" he screamed, not at all like the man we'd known thus far. "This is Hell Week! Get in the water! *Now!*"

Seeing this other side of Benelli shocked us. I knew we were headed back into the surf, but I didn't expect Benelli to be the one to send us there. As I rolled around in my Pacific hot tub, I tried to remember every girl I had ever kissed—the innocent first-grade kiss of Christina on the playground, the not-so-innocent high school kisses in the backseat of a car on a Friday night, and others. While I sat there reminiscing of good times, I shut out everything around me and hung a mental "Do Not Disturb" sign outside my door. If I'd been paying more attention to what was going on, I might've realized how bone cold I was.

A blur of guys rang the bell, but I tried not to let it affect me, to keep myself closed off. I might've started feeling sorry for myself if I didn't, but it was a challenge. Priest had been the first to ring out, and that demoralizing blow made this the second-worst moment of Hell Week for me. These were some of our toughest brothers, and now they were leaving. The good cop, bad cop routine had taken a monstrous bite out of us, and those who stuck it out were freezing our petunias off. I couldn't let it get inside my head or my heart.

After the bell ringing died, my classmates and I trudged out of the water to get hammered on land. The constant calisthenics clobbered us.

Finally, Instructor Benelli stopped the beach games. "Now I want each of your crews to turn your boat upside down and make a lean-to shelter facing away from the wind."

My crew and I propped the IBS up with our paddles and waited until Instructor Benelli came around to inspect us. "Now lie down under the boat with your heads near the closed end and your feet near the opening." Still shivering and wet, we complied, huddling up close to each other for body warmth. "I'm going to cover you with sand. This will give you insulation to help keep you warm." He shoveled generous amounts of sand on our bodies. "Now get some sleep. You're going to need it."

A moment later Martinez was already snoring. I was jealous that he'd fallen asleep so quickly and easily, and to add insult to injury, he made so much damn noise about it—*bastard*. I mentally shook my head and smiled. And that was all I remembered. Similar to that first short nap of Hell Week, I instantly moved into deep sleep. We slept for about one glorious hour. It was Wednesday night, and we had gotten a total of about two and a half hours' sleep since midnight on Sunday.

I awoke to Instructor Benelli's voice. "You know what time it is, gents."

We all stood groggily. Almost everyone seemed to have risen from a deep sleep—the light sleepers and nonsleepers either had evolved or were no longer with us. Our class was now about half the size it had been before we started Hell Week. I didn't feel that sense of dread in our class anymore, though. It was just another day in Hell Week. It was inescapable. We'd been forged into a steel band of brothers. We were a new, tougher, stronger class.

CHAPTER 22

Hyping Out

WE STOOD TOGETHER SHIVERING ON the beach after more surf torture in the cold Pacific Ocean—all of us except Petty Officer Lin, that is. He stood away from the rest of us again, not shivering this time but staring off into space. We all knew he had hyped out during the first half of Hell Week, before having to start his training over. "Hyping out" is what we call it when someone is in stage-three hypothermia. Stage one is mild to strong shivering with numbness in the hands—most people have experienced this level of hypothermia. Stage two brings violent shivering with mild confusion and stumbling, and in stage three, the core body temperature drops below ninety degrees, shivering stops, and a person becomes a babbling, bumbling idiot. There is no stage four, only death.

"Lin, get in formation!" one of our instructors yelled.

But instead of getting in formation, Lin staggered back toward the ocean. Another SEAL instructor speedily cut him off before he reached the water and then led Lin to the ambulance. Some of us started to follow to help him, but an instructor barked, "Stay in formation!" and we all obeyed.

The ambulance's lights flashed and siren blared as it sped away with Petty Officer Lin, taking him to Medical. We all stood there, holding our positions, but I had no doubt that we were all thinking the same thing: *I hope he's all right, but thank heavens that wasn't me.*

Medical had stripped off Lin's wet clothing, given him humidified oxygen, kept him under heat blankets and heat lamps in a warm compartment, injected him with warm intravenous fluids, and administered other treatments. He recovered but didn't return to Hell Week. Since he'd finished half of Hell Week with a previous class and half with my class, the instructors decided that two halves equaled a whole. Lin would rejoin my class after we completed Hell Week, and we were all thrilled at the news we hadn't lost him.

Now the instructors must have felt some relief knowing that they had whittled the group down to the guys who didn't know when to give up. They must also have felt a burden of responsibility, knowing that we were the mule-headed ones who might literally die trying to succeed.

CHAPTER 23

Black Knights

THURSDAY MORNING, LIKE EVERY HELL Week morning, the sunrise was incommensurably glorious. Its light and heat were unmatched by anything man could ever create as it took away the loneliness of darkness by illuminating other living people and things. The world became more vibrant, and the sun's radiance always seemed to lift the spirits of our class.

We upped our boats and headed east across Highway 75 to the mudflats of San Diego Bay. There we competed in the Mud Olympics, which included cartwheel races, fireman's-carry races, leapfrog races, snake races, three-legged races, and wheelbarrow races. Every step I took on every event sunk about a foot into the black slime. In the end, we looked like a bunch of chocolate Easter bunnies except for the whites of our eyes.

Later, we washed most of the mud off in the bay before we paddled our boats north to the NAB for more games, a hot lunch, and a trip to Medical at the Naval Special Warfare Center. Medical personnel examined us for serious injuries, including "flesh-eating bacteria." Actually, the bacteria release toxins that destroy skin and muscle rather than actually eating it. And since trauma covered our bodies from head to toe, we were meals on wheels for the killer bacteria. We should have enjoyed the break from the more strenuous activities, but most of us stressed more about being pulled from Hell Week for medical problems than doing push-ups 'til we dropped.

Even though we looked like the living dead, most of us acted as if we were perfectly healthy. It's like we were each channeling the persistent Black Knight in the British comedy *Monty Python and the Holy Grail*. The Black Knight fights King Arthur to stop him from crossing a bridge. The king cuts off the Black Knight's left arm, but the knight doesn't give up, saying, "'Tis but a scratch," and claiming, "I've had worse." The battle resumes, and King Arthur cuts off the Black Knight's right arm as well, but he continues to battle, armless and kicking at King Arthur. When the king tells him that he can't win with no arms, the Black Knight replies, "It's just a flesh wound." Like the Black Knight, we downplayed our weaknesses and persisted in the face of overwhelming odds, sometimes to the point of ridiculousness.

It seemed to work, though, because Medical cleared all of us to continue Hell Week, and we gave a collective sigh of relief.

CHAPTER 24

"You All Fail!"

THE BIGGEST SCARE OF HELL Week came after breakfast on Thursday morning. The SEAL instructors herded us into a warm classroom and sat us down. We stank like something out of the sewers—sweat, mildew, open sores, mud, seawater, seaweed, and piss. The stench kept the instructors at a distance as they handed out paper and pencils.

"Write down your Hell Week experience up until now, and do not fall asleep," one instructor said.

I started to write something, then caught myself nodding off. I ground my teeth and pushed myself onward, continuing to write. The room gradually grew darker, as if someone was using a dim switch on the lights. Our class officers and others fell asleep. Eventually, it became so dark that I couldn't even see what I was writing anymore.

An instructor tapped me on the shoulder from behind. When I turned around, he motioned for me to quietly leave the classroom.

About five of us, including our leading enlisted man, stood outside the classroom for a few minutes waiting for further orders.

Then an instructor's voice shouted from inside the classroom. "What are you people doing? You slept for five hours! The only way you can make up that time is to repeat Hell Week again! You all are going to fail! Get wet and sandy! Move, move, move!"

Suddenly, the sleepyheads came bursting outside in a panic, running to the surf. When they returned, they were wet and covered with a layer of sand.

"Instructor say we fail," Martinez sadly told me as he took his place beside me. "Must go Hell Week again!"

"It's not true," I said.

Our leading enlisted guy laughed. "You guys weren't asleep more than five minutes."

The sleepyheads looked like they wanted to believe us, hoped we were telling the truth, but they seemed skeptical. I don't know who was smarter: us for following orders and staying dry, or them for getting an extra five minutes of sleep. Either way, there was no time to dwell on it. The week wasn't finished.

CHAPTER 25

Around the World

THURSDAY NIGHT, WE RAN ANOTHER land race with our boats. And just as with most of our other races across land, my crew came in last and would have to make up time in the water. We launched from the Naval Special Warfare Center in hopes of catching the others in a trip "around the world." We would have to travel northwest through the Pacific Ocean, along the western shore of Coronado, around the tip of Coronado, southeast along the opposite shore of Coronado, and down into San Diego Bay.

As we paddled northwest, we quickly passed another boat crew. *One down, two more to go.* We passed the Hotel del Coronado, its light shining on the boulders we had cracked with our bodies earlier in the week.

As we swept along the dark sea, I saw someone walking across the water and nearly jumped out of my skin. "Did you guys see that?" I asked, pointing to the silhouette.

Martinez and the others didn't seem concerned.

Then the one person morphed into *three* as a black female musical trio shook its act on the water.

I blinked. "You really don't see that?"

"See what?" someone said.

I bit my lip and shook my head. "Never mind." I must've been hallucinating. Not surprising since we'd only gotten a total of about two and a half hours of sleep in the past four days. But at least I enjoyed the dance while it lasted.

We passed another boat. Half its crew looked like they were asleep.

One more boat to pass, and we could take the lead.

"Stop," someone said minutes later. "We've got to stop for the stoplight." No one responded, and then he laughed, realizing he, too, was seeing things. There couldn't possibly be a traffic light in the middle of the ocean! And even if there had been, why would we stop for it?

In truth, the moonlit ocean was quiet and peaceful. We stayed dry, and no instructors harassed us. We actually felt so comfortable that we sailed through the magical waters between consciousness and sleep.

Then . . . *bloop.*

Martinez toppled into the ocean. The cold splash quickly woke him up, and he sputtered before quickly righting himself and treading water.

"Man overboard," I said to the others.

Our response was slow, but we maneuvered the boat to him and assisted him back aboard.

As we rounded the northern part of Coronado, I was falling in and out of a light sleep when someone sat up straight and shouted. All of us groggily looked at him for a moment before we busted out laughing. The yeller laughed, too. No one asked him what he saw. Talking was too much of a burden.

We'd paddled southeast along the opposite coast of Coronado before I hallucinated again. This time, I saw a destroyer lit up like Christmas. The ship stretched over five hundred feet in length and probably displaced over eight thousand tons. It made me feel smaller than an ant floating on a turd in the toilet. The destroyer's foghorn let out a long deep belch that almost knocked us off our floating turd. It was no hallucination! The destroyer had just started moving in our direction, and we were passing in front of it. We snapped into hyperawareness and paddled for our lives.

The humongous ship sailed directly toward our starboard side. We paddled faster and faster until we cleared its path. Even then, we continued to paddle fast. Ensign Mark's boat was still somewhere out in front of us, and I didn't want to settle for second place.

After we paddled under Coronado Bridge, we approached Ensign Mark's boat. They were dead in the water. This was our moment. We could beat them.

"Come here, guys," Ensign Mark said.

We ignored him and paddled past.

Mark's boat crew all started shouting at us to stop.

"Hold up, hold up," our boat leader said. "Let's see what they want."

We all nodded and pulled up alongside them.

"One of our boat crews hasn't won one evolution during Hell Week," Mark said. "Let's give them this one."

We agreed. It paid to be a winner, sure, but the lowest ranking boat crew was bankrupt physically and mentally. Never winning a contest meant never catching a breather and always receiving extra punishment. They had suffered the worst in Hell Week.

We explained the plan to each of the other boats as they joined us in San Diego Bay. We let the losing crew take off at full speed, and we pretended to try and catch them. Unfortunately, the instructors saw through it, and we *all* became losers. After paying our debts, the instructors told us to prop up our boats as lean-tos again, and we got another hour of sleep.

CHAPTER 26

Treasure & Ghosts

It was still Thursday night when we began the Treasure Hunt. The instructors gave a different clue to each of the boat crews. My crew's first clue was "rubber duck."

After discussing the clue and figuring out where we were supposed to go, my crew headed off for the Special Boat Unit building with the IBS on our heads. There we found an instructor who told us that we had guessed the location of our first clue correctly. We were elated, and he gave us our next clue: "Milk Duds."

This one was trickier than the previous clue. We argued about where the next location was—the cafeteria, Explosives Ordnance Disposal Three (EOD Three) . . . We all had different ideas. We remained divided until our boat leader just made the call. "Let's go to the cafeteria," he said.

When we arrived at the cafeteria, we found out we were wrong and our next clue wasn't there. With our crippled bodies, we had to travel across the base again, with that heavy boat still on our heads, until we reached EOD Three, where we found our next clue.

Our performance got worse from there. We blew more and more clues, leading to more and more wandering, leading to more and more IBS bouncing on our heads and more and more asphalt beating our feet. The more we wandered, the lower our IQs dropped.

During Hell Week, that IBS reduced more than one strong man to tears. Sometimes the pain of that damn boat on my head was so bad that the only thing that kept me going was the hope that eventually I might black out.

But I never did. Instead, the other crews seemed to have finished. My crew's ghosts would probably still be wandering the Naval Amphibious Base today looking for clues if the instructors had not ended the Treasure Hunt. We never found our last clue.

CHAPTER 27

Demolition Delight

Friday morning, we paddled south to the demolition (demo) pits, located just north of the Silver Strand State Beach, which we'd claimed as Camp Surf. We crawled under barbed wire while artillery simulators whistled and exploded. Red and white smoke covered the area as machine guns blasted away.

A whistle blew. *Tweet.*

It was déjà vu.

We crossed our legs, covered our ears, and opened our mouths. *Tweet, tweet.* We low-crawled to the sound. I hated the whistle, but crawling on the sand didn't hurt nearly as much as crawling on the asphalt, like we did during Breakout on the first night of Hell Week.

Tweet.

Smoke, explosions, and gunfire continued to fill the air. We crawled to the demo pit, which was about one hundred feet across, six feet deep, and full of muddy seawater. Then we crawled in the mucky hole.

Navy SEAL Training Class 144

Two ropes stretched across the demo pit. With feet on the bottom rope and hands grasping the rope above our heads, we took turns crossing over the pit. Following tradition, every time one of us fell in the pit, the class said, "*So solly*," imitating World War II Japanese soldiers showing fake sympathy for our fallen frogmen. Thankfully, I, along with some of my classmates, made it across without falling in.

For our second crossing, the instructors raised the stakes by offering a break in training to anyone who could get across. They also raised the difficulty level by shaking the ropes. Each student who'd tried ended up taking a dip in the mud.

Then my turn came. Before Hell Week, I had set that class record for running the O-Course. *Obstacles are my thing*, I reminded myself. As I started across, the instructors shook the rope. I stayed on. An artillery simulator blew up nearby, sprouting a black fountain of mud. It didn't faze me. I continued across, and my classmates cheered me on.

When I got to the halfway point, the instructors really started yanking on the ropes. And the harder the instructors yanked, the harder I resisted. The ropes moved so violently that I had to stop in order to hang on with both legs and arms. I felt my strength begin to fade and knew I'd have to attempt to cross before losing all my energy. As I lifted one foot to take a step, the other leg and two arms weren't enough to maintain my hold. I fell into the mud pit with a spectacular splash.

Like Olympic judges at the high dive, Instructor Benelli and the other instructors held up their fingers with scores for each of our falls into the demo pit. We laughed, and the sun warmed me to the core. It felt good to have survived Hell Week so far. And despite our individual shortcomings, as a class we were doing a pretty damn good job. SEALs from Team One had even dropped by to congratulate us, saying they looked forward to operating with us someday. *Me, too*, I thought. *Me, too.*

CHAPTER 28

Bullet Train

It was some time in the afternoon that my classmates started talking like we were in the last day of Hell Week. I thought they were hallucinating again because a week is seven days, and this was only our fifth day. But it turned out I was the dumb ass when I learned Hell Week always lasted five and a half days, not a full seven. We were almost there.

For our next task, we ran with our boats from the Naval Special Warfare Center and hit the Pacific Ocean. My boat crew turbo-paddled north, passing everyone. When we landed on the beach and began land travel, that same boat pounded up and down on my same skull while the same ground jacked the same bones in my legs, and my same knees absorbed the same shock.

I pushed forward, even though my whole crew knew that Ensign Mark's long-legged crew would pass us on land. They always did. Our legs were just too short to compete. We had trained together enough to know which guys were strongest in which events. *Why bother trying if we already know the outcome? Losers always suffer. Why add even more suffering by trying?*

But something different happened this time. Suddenly, we weren't competing against Mark's crew or any other crew. We were competing against ourselves. The only thing worse than defeat was defeat without having spent everything trying. For the first time since the beginning of training, Smurf Crew rocketed over land. The exhilaration of it overpowered all my pain. We ran like a Japanese bullet train, boat rapidly bouncing high off our heads and sand flying from our heels. Without any words exchanged, we transcended ourselves. Nothing could catch us. Not pain, not fear, and especially not discouragement.

My crew was the first to arrive on the grinder inside the training compound. Instructor Benelli looked surprised to see us. "Good job. You guys really put out. Take a seat."

We lay down and used our boat like a giant pillow, resting our heads on it. Our makeshift rubber-pillow-and-asphalt bed sucked heat from the sun. It felt like sitting in a sauna at a resort as the sunshine kissed my face. I drifted in and out of a light sleep.

It pays to be a winner.

CHAPTER 29

Hell Week Is Secured

AFTER YET ANOTHER ROUND OF surf torture, shivering and dripping, we stood in a line formation facing the Pacific—ready to plunge into the cold, wet water again. We waited. For five and a half days, we'd performed over one hundred hours of calisthenics, ran more than two hundred miles, and did it all on no more than four hours of sleep.

"About-face," Captain Bailey commanded. He was the top SEAL at BUD/S, our commanding officer (CO).

In zombie form, we each did a one-eighty. Captain Bailey stood in front of us with Lieutenant Morris, Instructor Benelli, and some of our other instructors. Beside our CO was another man I didn't recognize.

"Captain Bailey," Ensign Mark said.

"Hooyah, Captain Bailey!" our class greeted him.

"This week, you made the impossible possible," Captain Bailey began. "You did something few people can do. In the future, if you ever start to feel sorry for yourself, *stop*.

Remember this great achievement and know that you can achieve more." He nodded to us. "Now I want to introduce our distinguished guest from NASA, Mr. . . . ." It was a long name that none of us seemed to understand, which was only compounded by sleep deprivation and walloping fatigue.

We must've said every letter in the alphabet, with some Ecuadoran Spanish pronunciation for good measure. "Hooyah, Mr. Alphabetsoupski!"

"Hell Week is secured," the NASA man said.

"Is this another trick?" someone asked.

"Is it really over?" came another voice.

"Hooyah!"

Some guys hugged each other, some cried, and some cheered. And some, like me, stood there in a stupid daze. At the time, I still thought Hell Week was seven days, so I couldn't figure out why we were being told it was already over. The instructors had to be screwing with us. But if what everyone was saying was true and Hell Week was finished, why was I still standing? How could I have possibly made it through Hell Week? It boggled my mind.

Some will find it difficult to believe, but in spite of all we had gone through, I hadn't thought about ringing the bell once. Later, I would hear Captain Bailey say that he, too, hadn't considered quitting Hell Week when he'd been a student. I could totally understand. Maybe most guys thought about quitting at some point during Hell Week, but I couldn't see how they could wrestle with that decision and then actually complete the week. It was all I could do to focus on surviving. I couldn't imagine having the extra mental or physical strength to debate myself.

I visually inspected myself, and my arms seemed swollen, so I touched them. Seawater oozed out as if I were a sponge. I had already begun to shed my outer skin like a molting snake—later, I would shed that whole outer layer of skin, just like all the other trainees.

"Try to focus on eating and sleeping," Instructor Benelli warned us. "If you get hurt and have to go to a hospital, go to our military hospital because the civilian doctors will probably freak out and put you in intensive care. The military doctors have treated us before, and they know what to do."

I looked down at my jungle boots. They had basically been new before Hell Week, and now the sides were ragged and the soles thin, as if I'd worn them a lifetime. The navy would issue us new ones. They'd have to. These things were going to fall off my feet at this point.

We traded our white T-shirts for brown T-shirts, signifying that we completed Hell Week. That simple brown shirt was the coolest thing I'd ever earned. Our class had also previously designed "Class Hell Week" shirts for those who finished, so now we could proudly wear them.

Instructor Benelli congratulated each one of us, and we stuffed our faces with pizza. Then we hobbled to our rooms. As we crawled into our racks to sleep, guards watched us in case any medical emergencies arose. I thought I'd sleep for two or three days, but I only slept about fourteen hours. But it was the best fourteen hours I'd had in what felt like forever.

CHAPTER 30

Hell Week Survival Tips—Believing

A LOT OF PEOPLE ASK ME for tips on getting through Hell Week, so I'll share the most important thing to help you get through "the week" and a lot of other things. *Believe strongly that you can accomplish the task.* It's a deceptively simple principle, but it's tough to master. In psychology, this is called "self-efficacy," a concept made famous by Dr. Albert Bandura.

Remember We Are Not Puppets

Psychologists and others often talk about influences of the mind and the environment as if we were puppets pushed by our brain and pulled by circumstance. We are *not* puppets. Through our behavior, we can influence our mind and environment. Just because we are born with a lower IQ, for example, doesn't mean we have to accept it. We can educate ourselves. We may be born into poverty, but we can attempt to get out. During Hell Week, an individual's capabilities often seem like they won't be enough, but the individual must perform anyway. The situations often seem impossible, but each person must succeed. How you behave in the face of those capabilities and the environment that is thrust upon you affects the outcome. The most important influence on your behavior is your belief system.

Believe Strongly

Believing strongly that we can achieve a task increases our chances of success. Strong belief leads to focus, effort, and persistence. This influences us to create specific, challenging goals. In order to achieve the goals, we break them down into manageable objectives, and to accomplish those objectives, we form strategies.

Focus, Effort, and Persistence

For example, just getting accepted to BUD/S is tough in itself—in my case, only one out of one hundred were accepted. Go to the Navy SEALs' official website (see appendix) and learn what preparation is needed. Then believe strongly you can do it. Again, it sounds simple, but it's not. It's easy to lose focus when there are so many other activities available—dating, video games, TV, Internet—when we should be doing our runs, push-ups, sit-ups, chin-ups, and swims. *Stay focused.*

It's easy not to give it your all on the workouts, but put forth the effort. It's tough to train every week, but persist.

Goals

Goals can be tricky. Vague goals lead to vague results. If the goals are too easy, we don't progress fast enough. If the goals are too difficult, we give up or injure ourselves before we get to the starting line. Goals have to be specific and challenging. Probably the most important goal for me in Hell Week was not to ring the bell. I may have gotten injured by Mother Nature or failed for some other reason, but I had total control over whether I rang the bell. I believed this so strongly that I didn't think once about ringing it during Hell Week. Other guys thought about ringing the bell but didn't. Some guys thought about the bell too much—and when their bodies started to break and the environment came crashing down on them, they rang out.

Objectives

Enduring Hell Week is just too big to comprehend. Break it down into small objectives. One evolution (activity) at a time. For example, a boat race. You don't even have to think about the whole boat race; just break it down to your individual responsibility—paddling. When the race is done, move on to the next objective. Thinking too much about what happened and what is about to happen will wear you down. Live in the moment, and take it one step at a time.

It really works. During one of my summer jogs in Okinawa, Japan, the sweltering heat was brutal and I desperately wanted to quit. But I knew I needed to do it, so instead of thinking about finishing the whole jog, I broke it down into smaller objectives: get to that tree up ahead. When I reached one tree, I set a new objective to make it to the next tree. Before I knew it, I'd completed the jog.

STRATEGIES

Use strategies to accomplish objectives more effectively. Strategic possibilities are endless, and not every strategy works for every person. But I'll cover a couple major ones that stood out for me at specific moments:

1. **Use your imagination.** Surf torture is challenging, and it happens often during Hell Week. Singing as a group is a great strategy for getting through surf torture in the beginning; however, be prepared for when the group breaks down—people quitting, fatigue, and so on. Prepare some images you can escape to when the cold comes calling. For me, although my body sat in cold water during Hell Week, mentally I sat alone in my hot tub. When that wasn't enough, I mentally sat in my hot tub and thought about additional pleasant memories. Although you shouldn't practice freezing yourself—catch hypothermia once and it's easier to catch hypothermia

again—it's helpful to practice some meditation now in preparation.
2. **Use your muscles effectively.** For runs, swims (with fins), and the obstacle course, I mainly used my legs and tried to let everything else relax. Because the thigh muscles are the biggest, I used them for power and the smaller calf muscles for balance. For paddling, again, I used the biggest muscles for power—my shoulders. The forearms were for balance.
3. **Compete with yourself.** It may seem impossible to keep up with the gazelles, or it may seem easy to fall back with the boys in the circus, but you are your own greatest competitor. If you compete with the gazelles and win, you're finished, but if you compete with yourself and win, you're never finished. There's always the next level. The more you compete with yourself, the faster you'll grow.
4. **Think positive.** If you catch yourself thinking a negative thought, change it into a positive one. For example, *Surf torture is going to suck* can easily be converted to *I can't wait to kick that ocean's ass when they stick us in the water again*. When you start to feel nervous about something, use that energy to empower yourself.
5. **Lighten up.** A little black humor goes a long way. Finding humor in the worst situations can help you and others. They say laughter is the best medicine for a reason.

6. **Be flexible.** You may think you made it to Wednesday night and the instructors are now your new buddies. You may think the hardest part is over. But that's when they kick you in the crotch. And you've got to pick yourself up and win the next event.

As I mentioned earlier, the most important thing you can do to get through challenges like Hell Week is to believe strongly that you can succeed. Without a strong belief, you ensure failure. With it, you are not guaranteed success, but your chances of success increase exponentially. Good luck!

CHAPTER 31

Go for the Blackout

COMPLETING HELL WEEK WAS NOT the end for most of us. We began a new way of thinking, a new way of living. Some men in our class couldn't continue training because of Hell Week injuries, particularly cellulitis and iliotibial band tendinitis (IBT). All of our bodies were swollen, but for those with cellulitis, the outer and inner layers of skin were actually infected. With IBT, the muscles and iliotibial bands drew too tight, pulling the joints out of alignment and causing them to rub against the knees and/or hips, resulting in additional swelling and pain.

Training slowly resumed after Hell Week, mostly with lots and lots of stretching. Then it picked up speed. Time limits tightened. Distances increased. More swims, runs, and obstacle-course completions. Academic tests continued, too. Enlisted men always had to score 70 percent or higher. Officers, 80 percent or higher. Our main subject of study after Hell Week was hydrographic reconnaissance.

An important evolution for me was the fifty-meter underwater swim. One day, at the pool, Instructor Benelli said, "All of you have to swim fifty meters underwater. You'll do a somersault into the pool, so no one gets a diving start, and swim twenty-five meters across. Touch the end and swim twenty-five meters back. If you break the surface at any time, you fail. Don't forget to swim along the bottom. The increased pressure on your lungs will help you hold your breath longer, so you can swim farther."

I lined up with the second group of four students. We cheered the first group on.

"Go for the blackout," some of us said.

When it was my turn, I hyperventilated to decrease the carbon dioxide in my body and decrease the drive to breathe. Then, during my ugly flop into the pool, I lost a lot of breath. I oriented myself and swam as low as I could. After swimming twenty-five meters, I neared the other side. During my turn, my foot touched the wall, but I didn't get a good push off.

My throat began to convulse as my lungs craved oxygen. *Go for the blackout*, I told myself. I swam as hard as I could, but my body slowed down. The edges of my vision began to gray until I found myself looking at my destination as if through a tunnel. When I felt myself begin to pass out, I actually felt peaceful. If I had any lingering fears of drowning, they were gone now. I tried to focus on the wall. Finally, my hand touched it.

An instructor grabbed me by the waistband of my UDT swim shorts and helped pull me out. I had passed. Some in our class failed, though. They would have a second chance later, but if they failed again, they would be dropped from training. It was important to remember that just because Hell Week was over, it didn't mean we could slack off.

CHAPTER 32

Shark Bait

ONE DAY, AS PART OF our hydrographic reconnaissance training, we rode in a patrol boat parallel to the beach. We would form a human line parallel to shore and swim toward land, stopping at regular intervals so each swim pair could drop a lead weight tied to the end of a thin rope. One guy recorded the depth on a Plexiglas slate while the other dove down and searched for enemy obstacles, reefs, or mines, which would also be recorded. Later, our class leaders would compile the swim pairs' information into a report and brief an instructor, who played the role of a commanding officer gathering intel before making an amphibious landing. Without such information, an amphibious craft might drop off its men, burdened with heavy packs filled with mission equipment, in a deep watery grave rather than shallow water. Or the amphibious craft may be stopped by a reef, allowing the enemy time to direct their fire at the men in the halted vessel.

My swim buddy and I kept low as we quickly crawled sideways into an IBS tied snugly to the seaward side of the patrol boat. I held on to my face mask with one hand and rolled off the speeding IBS into the ocean. If I hadn't held on to my mask, the impact of hitting the water at that velocity would've snatched it off my head. Training was high speed and better than any roller coaster.

In the water, the warmth and buoyancy of my wetsuit were my salvation as my classmates and I lined up parallel to the shore and swam in. When we reached a predetermined distance, we stopped. As instructed, I held on to a line attached to a lead weight and then dropped the weight. After it hit the seafloor, I counted the knots on the line to determine depth and recorded the information on my Plexiglas slate. Meanwhile, my swim buddy dove down and searched for obstacles. He found none, so I recorded that on the slate, too. We continued the process of gathering and recording data until we reached the shore.

Then we swam back out to sea where our extraction area was. There we got into line formation parallel to the shore again, spaced ourselves out at about twenty-five-foot intervals, and waited for the boat to return.

Somebody floated outside of formation.

"You're out of line!" we yelled to him.

The boat recovered us one by one. As it neared me, I kicked my feet hard, helping me rise out of the water. I lifted my arm closest to the boat high in the air, and a black elastic loop, held by a classmate in the IBS, ringed my arm. The force of the speeding boat transferred into the loop, slinging me into the back of the IBS. I scurried out of the IBS and onto the patrol boat.

Then the IBS ran over the head of the guy out of line.

It sure looked like it hurt, but he was still conscious and treading water like the rest of the guys still in the water. So we finished the end of the pickup, then swung around to pluck out the straggler. He was colder than the rest of us and had a knot on his head, but he was okay. Now he understood the importance of staying in line during the extract. I don't know how he survived it, but we had a good laugh. And he got some extra push-ups.

CHAPTER 33

Underwater Knot Tying

WEARING ONLY OUR UDT SHORTS, my classmates and I climbed fifty feet of stairs to the top of a water tank we called the "dive tower." Inside, it looked like a small circular swimming pool with a concrete walkway surrounding it, but this pool was fifty feet deep. I lowered myself into the warm water. I was instructed to dive down about fifteen feet and tie five knots into a circular trunk line secured to the inner walls of the tower: a becket bend (a.k.a. a "sheet bend"), a bowline, a clove hitch, a rolling hitch, and a square knot. These were some of the knots we would have to use for demolitions, so we had to be able to do them under all conditions. For example, the becket bend and square knot can be used for splicing the end of a detonating (det) cord. I'd learned most of the knots in Boy Scouts growing up, so I had no problem doing them, but this was the first time I'd be tying them fifteen feet underwater.

We could tie one knot for each of five dives, but I thought that five dives would be too tiring. As would one dive to tie all five knots. I didn't have the lungs for that. We could perform any combination of dives and knots we wanted, and I carefully selected mine.

I greeted the instructor, who was decked out in full scuba gear. "Respectfully request to tie the becket bend, bowline, and clove hitch." He gave me the thumbs-down, which indicated permission to descend into the water. I mirrored his thumbs-down, showing him that I understood. He gave me the sign again, and I made my combat descent fifteen feet below.

In Boy Scouts, I could tie the bowline with one hand in the dark, so being able to use both hands with my eyes open made it easier. Even if I was underwater. I tied the other two knots; then I gestured to the instructor, forming a circle with my index finger touching my thumb: *okay*. He checked the knots and gave me the okay signal back. I untied them and gave him the thumbs-up. He acknowledged, pointing his thumb up also, giving me permission to ascend.

On my second dive, I tied the last of the two knots and gave the instructor the okay sign. He didn't even seem to look at the knots. He just stared into my eyes. He was going to give me trouble. I gave him the thumbs-up to ascend again, but he just kept staring. The depth put pressure on my chest, and my lungs demanded air. I knew what the instructor was looking for, and I wouldn't give him the satisfaction. My instructors had taught me well. I had the power to control my level of stress.

I can ascend myself, or you can drag my body to the surface when I pass out and administer mouth-to-mouth. Either way, buddy. I will not show fear.

He smiled and gave me the up signal before I even came close to passing out. I wanted to shoot to the top, but I couldn't show any panic or anxiety. Plus, shooting to the top creates a splash on the surface that isn't tactical. I ascended as slowly as I could.

Pass.

CHAPTER 34

Ecuadoran Fast-Rope Technique

A T THE END OF PHASE One, our times for the four-mile run, two-mile open-ocean swim, and obstacle course had to be faster. When we entered Phase Two, those standards were tightened again. Phase Two was land warfare, which included covert infiltrations, sentry removal, handling agents/guides, gathering intelligence, snatching the enemy, performing searches, handling prisoners, shooting, blowing stuff up, and more.[4]

On the beach south of the Naval Special Warfare Center, we rappelled from the sixty-foot rappelling tower. Over my uniform, I wore H-gear (military suspenders) attached to my utility belt. I'd covered the shiny metal surfaces on my belt with olive-drab tape to eliminate shine and metallic noise. On my belt, I carried four ammunition pouches in front, a

---

4 At the time of publication, land warfare was taught in Phase Three of BUD/S training.

canteen behind each hip, and a first-aid kit on the small of my back. A black KA-BAR knife in a black, high-impact plastic sheath was attached to the belt over my left hip, opposite my rappelling hand, with a nylon strap.

Among other rappelling techniques, we practiced the fast-rope. It should have been painless. Wearing fast-rope gloves, I grabbed hold of the rope with both hands and slid down, using my boots to help slow my descent. My gloves smoked as they rubbed against the rope, but that was normal.

At the bottom, I looked up to see Duque, one of the Ecuadoran special-ops guys, go next. But all I saw was a streak when he burned into the ground. It was as if his hands and boots had never even touched the rope.

His body crumpled when he hit the sand. "Ayee!"

The instructors rushed to him.

"What was that?" our lieutenant—whom we secretly called Lieutenant Devil—shouted.

"In Ecuador, rope is very big," Duque said, clutching his injured back. Both ropes were probably similar in strength, but the thinner American rope just slipped through his hands.

Devil just shook his head.

Upon completing our rappels, we did push-ups. The bottoms of my jungle boots, which I had modified earlier in training, entered Devil's crosshairs. "What are those boots?"

"I paid a cobbler to take out the steel shank and put better soles on, sir," I explained. In Vietnam, more than one American soldier fell into a punji pit, a camouflaged hole in the ground with wooden stakes smeared with human feces (to increase infection) poking up from inside. The steel shank protected the foot against punji sticks, but since there weren't any punji sticks on the beaches of Coronado, I had taken the metal shank out. The jungle boot soles had been okay, but I'd thought black running soles would have been better so I had them redone. I'd gotten the idea from the same ensign who I'd gone with to have the zippers taken out of our trousers and replaced with Velcro before Hell Week began. As trainees, we were always looking for a competitive edge. This mind-set continues on into the teams, similar to how SEAL Team Six used stealth helos to raid bin Laden's compound.

This was my first opportunity to try the boots, and I loved them.

"Well, I don't want to see those boots tomorrow. Get wet and sandy."

I did as commanded, and much to my chagrin, I never wore my modified jungle boots in training again. At least Duque's back healed, and he stayed with our class. It was disappointing to see the ban of my secret boot modifications, but it was a relief to never see the Ecuadoran fast-rope technique again.

CHAPTER 35

Dazed and Confused

B RAND-NEW BUD/S BARRACKS HAD BEEN erected near the million-dollar condos on Coronado beach, and my class had been the first to christen them. Now there were only two men to a room, like a college dorm, and my new roommate and I shared a bathroom with another two-man room. Our class nicknamed the barracks the "sex palace" because of the steady flow of women who came at all hours, even as the days became longer and the nights shorter.

One Sunday, at about 1400 hours, my roommate and I finished cleaning our equipment. "I think I'm going to take a nap," I said.

"Good idea," my roommate said.

We retired to our racks, and after our little nap, my roommate and I woke up. The clock, which was in standard time, not military time, read six o'clock. *That little nap lasted four hours!* We hadn't realized how tired we were, but the nap felt almost as good as the long sleep right after Hell Week.

"Hurry, get into formation!" Ensign Mark called from outside. I tilted my head, confused. It was Sunday night. We were off duty.

Then somebody yelled our names. I hurried to the window and looked out. Another classmate ran past our room in uniform with his backpack on.

"What the hell is going on?" I asked.

Then it dawned on me: it was *Monday morning*! We hadn't even heard the alarm clock! Off flew our civilian clothes and on went our uniforms.

"Templin!" someone from outside shouted.

My roommate and I showed up in formation with our utility belts unbuckled, backpacks dangling, shirts and trousers unbuttoned, and shoes untied. We weren't the only ones, though. Others straggled into formation after us.

"We're going to have to skip breakfast," Ensign Mark said, "or we'll be late for the bus."

We took a navy bus out to the Naval Special Warfare Group One Mountain Warfare Training Facility located in the Laguna Mountains, roughly eighty-five miles northeast of our base in Coronado. A lot of guys slept during the ride, but my roommate and I didn't need to after that "nap."

After we reached the training facility and got our orders, we soon found ourselves rappelling down a mountain. The first guy practically slid straight down, scraping his body on the rocks. When he reached the painful bottom, instead of giving him bandages, the instructors gave him push-ups. Others rappelled correctly, bodies horizontal, backs facing the ground, and still others walked or hopped down the cliff face.

I prepared to take my turn. "Rappel on!" I said. Then I jumped out as far as I could, trying to reach the bottom in one jump.

As soon as I hit the peak of my flight, I felt weightless. And uneasy. It pays to be a winner, but it also pays to stay alive.

Gravity brought me back to the mountain, and I tried to land on my feet, not on my nose. When my jungle boots hit the mountain face, though, pain shot through my bones. Luckily, after that first leap, it only took one small hop to reach the ground.

"Rappel off!" I said.

The instructor on belay seemed to catch his breath after nearly witnessing a trainee die on his rope.

But Lieutenant Devil ate it up. "Great rappel!"

I sighed in relief and moved on to my next task.

CHAPTER 36

Spiderman vs. the Devil

On another day at the Naval Special Warfare Group One Mountain Warfare Training Facility, we were doing our land-navigation exercise. I lined up my compass on the map and started orienting myself.

Martinez snatched the map away from me.

I had done orienteering in the Boy Scouts and in high school army JROTC class, so I wasn't great, but it's not like I was a beginner. "What?"

"Not difficult." He pointed to a contour on the map. "We are here." He moved his finger to the destination on the map, then the trees to the east. "This is there. We go there." Without using a compass, he somehow walked us through the first part of the course as easy as if he were following street signs.

After the orienteering, we sat under trees in the shade eating our meal ready-to-eat (MRE) lunches.

Lieutenant Devil looked down at the ground. "Everyone lie down and take a break," he ordered as he picked up whatever he'd been staring at.

We did as instructed.

I stole a glance over at the Devil, and he was placing a spider—a big daddy longlegs—on a student, who showed a little nervousness but not enough of a reaction to satisfy the Devil. He took it back and put it on someone else, who started squirming and shaking.

"I hate spiders," I muttered.

Lieutenant Devil's ears perked up.

Here he comes.

Lieutenant Devil put the spider on my forehead.

I kept as still as I could, waiting for the insect's next move. In military march, we step off with our left foot, but the spider stepped off with its first right leg. Then its second left leg. All eight of its legs were so long and thin that they seemed to tremble as the spider moved down my face, tickling my eyebrows. It stopped, and its peanut-shaped body hovered above the bridge of my nose.

Devil's eager eyes opened wide.

I watched the spider anxiously as it stepped on my lips.

Keep moving, keep moving.

When its abdomen was over my mouth, I steeled myself, opened wide, and inhaled, sucking in the daddy longlegs. Then I closed my mouth and took a couple of bites before swallowing. The bitter taste was worth the price of helping the Devil's next victim. And well worth the look on Lieutenant Devil's face. His eyes went blank, as if he couldn't figure out how the magician had sawed the lady in half. Then the curtains closed early, and he sat alone in the dark with his little ticket stub.

Cracks of laughter broke among my classmates.

"Did he just eat that?" asked Doc.

"He's a freak of nature," Instructor Barnett said.

Lieutenant Devil tried to recover. "Find me another spider. All of you."

We went through the motions of beating around in the bushes for a while. Of course, no one was dumb enough to find him another spider.

CHAPTER 37

Snake Eater and Mud Sucker

ONE SUNNY AFTERNOON WE PRACTICED immediate action drills (IADs)—specifically, how to move and shoot as a SEAL squad of seven or eight men. My squad was made up of the same guys in my boat crew, and Martinez walked the point as we patrolled through the woods. I brought up the rear as assistant patrol leader, a machine gunner in front of me and rear security behind.

"Snake," Martinez said, stopping us midpatrol. "Dangerous." He picked it up from the trail with his bare hands and killed it to protect the rest of us.

Amazed and grateful, we proceeded forward again.

"Why'd you stop?" Instructor Barnett asked when we completed our patrol.

"Snake hurt squad," Martinez said. "Snakebite very bad."

He pointed to where the snake lay dead on the ground.

"All right, then," Instructor Barnett said, clearly impressed. "Go get some grub."

After dinner, we prepared for night operations. Lusting hands competed to grab the M16s and ammunition blanks lying on a long table. I saw two M14s all alone, waiting for someone to ask them to dance. The M14 was older, heavier, and not nearly as sexy as the M16, and an M14 magazine only held twenty rounds—ten less than the M16. But while the M16 danced like a girl with its smaller 5.56-millimeter rounds, the M14 danced like a *woman*, firing the bigger 7.62 millimeter. And there was enough ammo stacked around her to party all night long.

Once we had our weapons, my squad patrolled through the night to reach our objective. Suddenly, someone shot at us. They were only firing blanks, but we were trained to act like they were real. The rate of fire was slow and sporadic. We decided to wax the shooter, so we leapfrogged forward to his position. Four of us laid down cover fire while three rushed forward and dropped into position. Then the three in front fired at the threat while the four rushed up and dropped into position. We would continue leapfrogging until we eliminated the threat.

Suddenly, our left and right flanks opened up, unleashing heavy firepower on us. The enemy had sucked us into an ambush. We quickly leapfrogged back the way we had come, retreating. My squad members' M16s went *pop* while my M14 went *boom boom*. The sound of my firepower alone seemed to drown out the sound of the enemy. Combined with the firing of my fellow squad members, the ambushers became the ambushees.

Upon breaking contact with the enemy, we proceeded toward our objective.

Lieutenant Devil stopped us. "Who was the guy with the M14 shooting off like the Fourth of July?"

"Me, sir," I said proudly.

Lieutenant Devil opened the empty magazine pouch on my belt. "You used most of your ammunition before you even reached the objective! What will you do when you get there? Spit on them?"

The M16 ammo had been limited, but since I was the only one with an M14 and there were piles of ammo, I had left nothing on the table. I pulled magazines full of ammo out of my magazine pouches, shirt pockets, front trouser pockets, back trouser pockets—like a never-ending stream of silk scarves out of a magician's hat. I could've kept shooting until sunrise and still had rounds to spare.

Lieutenant Devil stared at me for a moment. "Drop down and push 'em out!"

I dropped down and did my push-ups. In a mud puddle.

CHAPTER 38

Why Birthdays are Kept Secret

WITH THEIR MIDDLE-AGED GUTS, INSTRUCTORS Barnett and Doc didn't look like any SEALs from the movies. The two looked like they'd have a hard time running the width of a soccer field. But those guys ran us all over Southern California. If they'd had a little more time, they would've run us to Argentina and back.

In contrast, our SEAL proctor was as weak as he looked. He served as a liaison between us and the other instructors and was definitely not the poster boy for physical fitness. One morning at the Naval Special Warfare Center, he led us in PT. He started out with jumping jacks. Then push-ups. His face turned red, and he broke out in a sweat as he worked along with us. Five minutes into the workout, he looked about to pass out. He stumbled off the dais and disappeared.

We stood there dumbfounded. *Now what?* Another instructor appeared and took over the PT. It was our proctor's first PT with us and his last. And he never ran with us, either.

But one day, we strolled into the classroom. A piece of paper lay in the middle of my path. I stepped around it. Someone behind me stepped on the paper, and it popped like a firecracker. *Bang!* Another guy sat down. *Bang!* A lone book lay on a desk. The guys passed it around carefully, as if it might be booby-trapped, until someone opened it. *Bang!*

Then our proctor walked in and stood at the front of the room. "Welcome to Demolitions 101."

He may have been a wimp, but he was the Stephen Hawking of explosives.

After three and a half weeks of land-warfare training at Coronado, we flew sixty miles over the Pacific Ocean to continue training on San Clemente Island. *Where no one can hear you scream.* Toward the end of the first week there, we received some good intelligence that it was our proctor's birthday. Birthdays are a carefully guarded secret in the teams. Nobody wants to be on the receiving end of birthday wishes from SEALs.

We were in a multipurpose room, checking our weapons, when someone said, "Let's do something special for him."

"Let's throw him in the surf," another guy suggested.

"Yeah," we agreed.

"Who'll give the signal?"

"I'll say 'happy birthday,'" Ensign Mark said. "And then we grab him."

There were nods of agreement all around.

Minutes later, our proctor walked in, and Ensign Mark gave the signal. "Happy birthday."

I jumped forward and grabbed our proctor around the lower legs, immobilizing him.

He looked down at me with a face that said, *What the hell?*

And none of my classmates moved to assist . . .

A bad feeling swept over me, like the rappel when I almost painted the Laguna Mountains with my blood. *Is everyone suddenly chicken? Did I misunderstand something?* Not a good idea to try taking down a SEAL from the front in the light of day with no backup.

The others leaped into action, thank heavens, taking the pressure off me. Our proctor didn't put up a fight. We carried him to the beach and threw him in the ocean with all his clothes still on. He stood up drenched from head to toe.

"Hooyah! Happy birthday!" we cheered.

He just smiled at us. All's fair in love and SEAL birthdays.

CHAPTER 39

Fire Team Templin

WE PREPARED TO SHOOT UP the range at San Clemente Island and fire a light M60 (M60E3), the same machine gun Sylvester Stallone used in *Rambo: First Blood Part II*. The instructors advised us to fire in bursts of three to five shots. Lying down in the prone position with the M60 mounted on a bipod, I shot down the first target, a black silhouette. I immediately attacked the second target in my lane. No sooner had the second gone down and I was already shooting the third. I hadn't paused between targets, so I ended up firing about a seventeen-round burst. After that, I shot at grass using three- to five-round bursts until I spent my fifty-round belt of ammunition.

And that was a problem. Although I'd controlled all my three- to five-round bursts, I'd fired the bursts in such fast succession that it looked like I'd ignored the instructors' instructions and fired everything on full auto like a raving lunatic.

When all the shooters had finished, Lieutenant Devil came up to me. "Great job, Rambo. Now, instead of a fifty-round belt of ammunition, we're gonna give you a two-hundred-round belt. And instead of shooting from the prone position with a bipod, I want you to stand and shoot one-handed—like Rambo. And I don't want you to stop shooting until all two hundred rounds have been fired." He gave me that evil grin that seemed to say, *Your pain is my pleasure.*

"Yes, sir," I replied. I didn't know if I could hold the light M60 one-handed, let alone shoot it one-handed. Rambo was Hollywood, but this was for real.

Instructor Barnett looked uneasy. This could be dangerous. He linked four fifty-round ammo belts together to create the two-hundred-round belt.

I loaded the first round into the M60. The instructors and my classmates watched me stand alone with the snake of ammo draped over my left forearm. My right hand held the M60 near my hip.

"The range is hot," an instructor said, giving me the go-ahead to shoot.

I pulled the trigger. The M60 tried to rise up and to the right on me, but I pulled it down and to the left, directing it at the silhouettes in my lane. Every fifth bullet burned white phosphorous—tracer rounds. One target went down in my lane. Then the next. And the next. I still had a lot of ammunition left. Pure ecstasy.

Since none of my classmates were firing in the lanes next to me, I blasted down the three silhouettes in the lane to my left. The white phosphorous rounds had lit the dry grass near the targets on fire, and smoke rose. Then I took out two targets in the right lane before my two hundred rounds of excitement finally ran out. I had concentrated so hard that the whole process seemed like it took a while, but it only lasted about one single minute. I put down the machine gun and made it safe, though the barrel literally glowed from the heat.

Lieutenant Devil and his instructors just looked at me without saying anything. Surely they had something to say. They always did. And my classmates grinned.

I couldn't understand their reactions. If I could do it, couldn't anyone? At the time, I still hadn't realized my special talent. Then somebody called me Fire Team Templin. A fire team is typically made up of three to four shooters, but I was just me. The nickname stuck.

CHAPTER 40

Platoon

"THE ADMIRAL WANTS TO GO on a ten-mile run with you guys," Lieutenant Devil said.

We were busting our humps every day in BUD/S, and the admiral wanted to go on a fun run with us? Some fun. None of my classmates or I were pleased in the least. *F-ing admiral.*

But we didn't have a choice. We loaded up in the trucks and headed out. During the ride, we grumbled. The admiral would probably be wearing a colorful headband, T-shirt, shorts, and expensive running shoes. This would be his only run for the day. We wore green caps, green long-sleeved shirts, green trousers, and jungle boots—an extra run added on to the beginning of our runs for the day.

F-ing admiral.

We arrived at the back of a building complex I'd never seen before, and the trucks stopped. We unloaded.

Standing next to a garbage Dumpster, Doc briefed us. "The lieutenant says this is the most realistic movie he's seen about the Vietnam War."

Lieutenant Devil had been an enlisted SEAL in Vietnam and later became an officer. Older than most navy lieutenants, SEAL lieutenants with enlisted experience were a special breed. Those with combat experience were priceless. So if he said it was realistic, it was *realistic*.

We quietly filed through the emergency exit of a building, where we entered what looked like a base movie theater. Inside, we took our seats, amazed that our ten-mile extra run had turned into a morning matinee.

Soon, the lights went out, and cans of Budweiser beer appeared. "One each. A gift from Stanley," a classmate said. Stanley was our cook, and maybe the beers really were from Stanley, but maybe they were from Lieutenant Devil . . .

I wasn't a drinker, so I gave mine to Schumann, a classmate sitting to my right. "Really?" His eyes and smile nearly popped off his face, and he looked like he'd "love me long time." Trainees weren't allowed to have booze in the barracks, and on the island we'd been isolated in training for days. As Schumann downed the first beer, I wondered if I'd have to carry him out of the theater later.

A quotation from the Bible appeared on the movie screen: "Rejoice, o young man, in thy youth." Then what looked like Vietnam appeared. Dead soldiers' corpses were zipped into body bags and loaded onto a plane. A new guy, Chris, walked past a combat vet who had that thousand-yard stare. Chris and his platoon rode a helicopter off to somewhere near the Cambodian border, and the movie began, filled with combat, treachery, and bravery.

Bits and pieces of the film burned into my consciousness. "I love this place at night," Sergeant Elias said. "The stars . . . There's no right or wrong in them. They're just there."

Later in the movie, another member of the platoon, Sergeant Barnes, shot Sergeant Elias, but Elias survived and tried to reach the extraction. When the platoon deduced that Barnes had killed Elias, they wished death on Barnes.

"Death?" Sergeant Barnes asked. "What do you all know about death?"

Finally, during a bloody battle with the Vietcong, Chris killed Sergeant Barnes. For Chris's wounds, he received a helo flight out of Vietnam.

"The war is over for me now, but it will always be there, the rest of my days," Chris said. Then Samuel Barber's "Adagio for Strings" played.

Platoon impacted me emotionally and spiritually. When the final credits rolled, with the lights still off, we quietly slipped out through an emergency exit. There were no hooyahs. Only reverence.

I still looked forward to serving in combat someday. I think we all did; it's what we were training for. And I guessed the Devil would probably win some battles against me, but when it mattered most, I hoped God would win my soul.

CHAPTER 41

Freak of Nature

ONE EVENING OUT AT SAN Clemente Island, someone had raided the galley. When the instructors found out in the morning, they started asking around to find out who did it.

Nobody seemed to know.

So Petty Officer Lin said he did it, even though he didn't. The instructors thought Lin was a great guy for taking the responsibility for someone else's sin, but one of my classmates mumbled that Lin was a kiss-ass.

No matter. We would all pay.

And how did the instructors make us pay? Usually by making us "get wet."

As they discussed the problem, my classmates gathered around. Meanwhile, I slipped away, ducking into the barracks and grabbing one of my uniforms. I ran outside to one of the fresh water sinks and opened the water faucet full blast, holding my uniform under the stream until it was completely wet. Then I wrung out the excess liquid. When the instructors actually told us to get wet, I slipped back into the barracks, stripped off my dry uniform, and put the "wet" uniform on over my dry body and dry underwear.

I remained in the barracks while my classmates ran to the ocean and jumped in. When they returned to prepare their gear for the next evolution, I blended in with the confusing rush of bodies, my uniform appearing as wet as theirs. After assembling our gear, we gathered in formation outside and double-timed to the shooting range.

As the noon sun reached its height and we continued shooting, my uniform had dried out, like magic, while everyone else's was still damp. And mine didn't have the salt residue from the seawater. I was a little worried—my uniform had dried out *too* fast.

"Templin, did you get wet?" Lieutenant Devil asked.

"Yes, sir."

He scratched his head. "How'd you get dry so fast?"

"I don't know, sir."

"Son, you're a freak of nature."

It was hard to hide my smile as I went back to shooting.

CHAPTER 42

Zombie Applause

WE PACKED WEEKS OF TRAINING into days. The brutal demands wore us down physically and mentally. One afternoon, my class stood outside looking like a platoon of zombies.

One of the guys had to carry a heavy pallet up a hill and back to repent for some earlier sin he'd committed. As he returned to the training compound, he was so worn out that he had no energy left in him, and he dropped the pallet in the dirt. Even though he still had to take the pallet across the compound and return it to where it was stored, he couldn't even grip the wood strongly enough to drag it.

Lieutenant Devil looked at our class. "Give him a hand."

We stared at Devil for a moment with those blank, zombie-like expressions on our faces. Someone clapped, and we all followed, bursting into spontaneous applause.

The lieutenant shook his head as if to say, *How can the whole class not understand me?*

Doc and Instructor Barnett laughed, and we stood there, not understanding what Devil was shaking his head at and what Doc and Instructor Barnett were laughing about.

Doc spoke simply and slowly, so our zombie minds could understand. "No. Help him *pick up the pallet* and take it over there."

The guys and I snapped out of our stupor and helped carry the pallet to the pile.

CHAPTER 43

Deliverance

If one of us got in trouble, Lieutenant Devil would often speak in a thick southern drawl, using a chilling reference from the movie *Deliverance*: "Get on down and root like the hog you are, boy." We'd have to get down on all fours and push dirt with our foreheads and snort like pigs.

One day, Lieutenant Devil said, "Templin, you look like that banjo-playing hillbilly kid in *Deliverance*."

Then, over the camp loudspeakers, someone played "Dueling Banjos," and Devil told me to dance. I did my best to dance a jig, and he loved it.

Never a dull moment.

CHAPTER 44

How the Chaplain Chipped My Tooth

I DON'T REMEMBER WHAT I DID, but it was probably something pretty stupid, like a firearm safety violation or a safety violation with explosives, and I likely deserved the punishment. For small violations, guys took a "flight," meaning they grabbed a small pallet, carried it across their back like airplane wings, ran to the top of a hill, and returned. More serious transgressions earned the heavier pallets, and the most serious of sins earned the dreaded Chaplain.

The Chaplain was a life-sized dummy that weighed about two hundred pounds. Running him up that hill was a killer. Once, one guy dropped the Chaplain and had to start over. Another got to the top of the hill, leaned against a large boulder for a rest, and was forced to do it again. Both guys were bigger than me.

Even so, I knew that someday I might have to carry a teammate out of danger, and the enemy wouldn't make excuses for me. So I carried the Chaplain in a fireman's carry. It was impossible to run. I had to move forward at a quick trot. Soon, my thighs and shoulders were burning, and as I neared the top of the hill, my shoulders went numb. On the way back down the hill, it took all my concentration to keep from falling face-first in the dirt.

Finally, I returned to the training compound. "Request permission to secure the Chaplain."

"Secure," an instructor said.

As I tried to lower the Chaplain, I collapsed. The Chaplain and I took a nosedive, and his helmet caught me in the mouth, chipping my front tooth.

Doc looked at my mouth and was concerned about permanent nerve damage, so he told me I'd have to leave San Clemente Island to get it fixed.

I was more worried about missing training than my tooth. "Can I continue training?"

"You'll only miss a day or so."

Lieutenant Devil nodded. "When you finish with the dentist, Templin, I want you to go to the armory and practice reassembling weapons."

"Yes, sir."

The next morning, I took the first flight out. On the mainland, at the navy dental center, the dentist capped my tooth so expertly that there was no noticeable difference between the white cap and my own pearly whites.

After eating a leisurely lunch with my patched-up tooth, I went to the armory and checked out some toys, as instructed. At the time, one of the more exotic weapons in the armory was the MP5N submachine gun. Created for the SEALs, it had a collapsible stock, tritium-illuminated front sight post, and a threaded barrel that we mounted a Knight's Armament Company sound suppressor on. I worked with it a little but then spent most of my time with the M60 machine gun because, for me, it was one of the more complicated weapons to reassemble.

In the evening, I spent a quiet meal in the cafeteria on Coronado's Naval Amphibious Base. Afterward, I went to bed early, savoring a long night's sleep.

When I flew back to San Clemente Island the next morning, the guys gathered around me.

"Did you get laid?" someone asked.

"No," I said.

"Did you get drunk?"

"No."

"Well, did you go to McDonald's?"

"No."

They walked away shaking their heads in disappointment. I felt like a square.

Then Lieutenant Devil asked, "Did you go to the armory and reassemble weapons like I told you?"

"Yes, sir."

"I know." Lieutenant Devil looked like he didn't know whether to be happy I followed orders or unhappy because he hadn't caught me slacking.

I couldn't understand the problem. I had done what I wanted to and loved it. I'd eaten delicious meals in the cafeteria, played with all the weapons in the SEAL training armory, and had a long, quiet sleep. I was living my dream.

CHAPTER 45

Quick Kill

TO FIRE WEAPONS LONGER DISTANCES, we needed to align the target in our front and rear sights. When things got up close and personal, we practiced the "quick kill," aligning the target in our front sight only and firing two shots into the enemy's chest.

"Smooth is fast," Instructor Barnett said. "Ensign Mark, I'm challenging your class to a showdown. Nine-millimeter pistols. Eight shots, eight targets. Choose your best shooter."

"Templin," Mark said.

I blinked. Why did my name come up? In a group of such outstanding classmates, it didn't make sense to me. Even so, I was honored and accepted the challenge.

Instructor Barnett's pistol was customized, and, of course, he was an experienced SEAL who'd been to the top military and civilian shooting schools. I had a pistol straight from the factory, and I was just a trainee.

My classmates and the other instructors silently watched as four black metal plates on top of a rack and four below were set up. *Bang, bang, bang, bang*—one, two, three, four. Barnett knocked down the top plates. Then he went to the bottom four targets. *Bang, bang, bang, bang*—one, two, three, *miss.*

He missed his last target.

I took a deep breath. I couldn't miss a single shot. I focused, aligned my sights, and took my eight shots. No misses. My class roared with applause.

Instructor Barnett had taught me well, and he should've just let it go. But instead of giving me a proud compliment, he said, "Well, when you go up against someone who's handicapped, you have a natural tendency to take it easy on him."

Some guys rolled their eyes and others grinned.

Lieutenant Devil just smiled his devious smile—he loved when others got taken out of their comfort zones, even his instructors.

It pays to be a winner.

CHAPTER 46

Saying Good-bye

WHILE I WAS A GOOD shooter, I struggled with demolitions studies. Effectively blowing up a bridge involves a good deal of math—my weakest subject—and academic failure would mean a swift kick out of BUD/S. After each demolitions test I came closer to failing. Too close for comfort.

So one evening, while my classmates slept, I studied for my next demolition test by the beam of my flashlight. I'd stayed in the game this long, and there was no way I would go down without a fight. When I finished studying, I grabbed a couple of hours of sleep.

That morning, we filed into a shack we called the "schoolhouse" to take our test. This was one of the toughest tests we'd taken, and though my head was groggy from the lack of sleep, I felt I'd prepared as much as possible.

When the results came back, the instructors started reading out the high scores first. Of course, our class officer,

Ensign Mark, MIT graduate, had one of the top scores. And so did I.

Lieutenant Devil pulled me aside. "You've been scraping by on almost every demolitions test—how'd you do it?"

I told him how I'd stayed up late and studied hard for it.

The corners of his mouth turned up. For every challenge, no matter how impossible, I found a way. We all did.

The next morning, I kneeled down like I did every morning and said a prayer. "Please help me do my best." Every morning of BUD/S I said those same words, and every morning I meant it with all my heart, but this morning I had a strong feeling that something was different.

It's time to leave here.

A crystal-clear calmness came over me. So many times I had fallen down, but He'd always picked me up. I was grateful for the opportunity to have come as far as I did.

In my mind, it didn't make sense. I passed my demolitions test with flying colors, earned pistol- and rifle-expert awards. I'd finished Hell Week without a thought of quitting and knew I could do more.

But even though it didn't make sense, I followed that feeling. I went to see our class proctor.

"Request to withdraw from training," I said.

He gave me a puzzled look. "Okay."

We walked over to see Lieutenant Devil. The proctor left us alone. Lieutenant Devil looked over my file. "You entered BUD/S because you wanted to fight terrorists?"

"Yes, sir."

He smiled approvingly. Then he filled out the paperwork. And it was over.

No one asked me to ring the bell. If they had, I might've stayed. Ringing the bell would've been extremely hard for me, maybe too hard.

Word traveled fast that I'd withdrawn from training. Before eating lunch, like everyone else, I did my pull-ups outside the cafeteria. Some instructors and students had quizzical looks on their faces. *Why is he doing something he doesn't have to do anymore?* Others hadn't heard the news yet and thought nothing of it.

I loaded up my tray with food one final time, and choosing to sit alone, I kept my chin up. I felt awkwardness but not shame.

Back in the barracks, I packed my sea bag. Then I got in the truck and the proctor drove me away. Watching the camp disappear in the side mirror, I felt a vague sadness.

"Feels like leaving brothers," I said.

I flew back to Coronado. At the Special Warfare Center, Master Chief Knepper looked at my file, then asked, "Why do you want to leave us?"

"I don't know, Master Chief."

"You should stay."

If Lieutenant Devil had pressed me, he might have been able to talk me into staying. The lieutenant might have convinced me it was all a brain fart. Now I had already committed myself. And the SEALs had taught me to hold my ground. The master chief and I went back and forth until he gave up.

I returned gear, received a medical check, and filled out paperwork. When Class 144 came back from San Clemente Island, I met up with my good buddies, the Ecuadoran commandos. They said that two more of my classmates left the island. Both rang the bell. (Later, one would have a change of heart and would be allowed to return to training.) On one of the last evenings out at the island, probably out of tradition, my class did a skit to entertain the instructors. They reenacted the pistol showdown of the eight plates between Instructor Barnett and me. Martinez and Duque said I should've talked to them before I left and that Lieutenant Devil said he didn't know why he'd let me go and wished he had stopped me.

I never found such a tight brotherhood again.

After BUD/S, I frequently dreamed I returned to Hell Week. Sometimes it sucked to be doing "the week" again. Sometimes my spirit flew at the joy of being back in the game. The dreams occurred so frequently that I finally recognized them for what they were—images of the past. And then the dreams stopped for the most part.

In Class 144, I think a couple of guys who probably should've stayed in training quit. And a couple of guys who probably should've quit had stayed. But I think that for the most part, those who became SEALs did the right thing.

I've often reflected on my decision to leave. What if I had the choice to make again? Would I do the same thing?

In the years since I left, I became a missionary for two years in Japan, earned a PhD in education (which was more difficult than Hell Week), lectured as a tenured professor for fourteen years, and achieved my childhood dream of becoming a best-selling author. My most treasured experiences are those with my wife and children. If I had stayed in the navy, I probably would've missed many family birthdays, Thanksgivings, Christmases, school events, and other special family occasions. Such sacrifices tear apart numerous marriages and families. It's a sacrifice that our men and women in the military uniform make every day, and it's a noble one. Although I feel some selfishness for enjoying the life I have, I feel strongly that I took the path I was supposed to take, and I would never change that.

During BUD/S training, my classmates and I had the honor of meeting the retired admiral James Stockdale, who said something that I would never forget. Although Stockdale had never been a SEAL, he was a special friend of the SEALs—one of the most decorated officers in the navy's history—and embodied all that is good about the navy. He once said, "Do the right thing even if it means dying like a dog and there's no one there to see you do it."

I agree.

CONTINUE TO END FOR EXCERPT OF
TRIDENT'S FIRST GLEAMING...

Appendix: How to Get to BUD/S

Visit

THE FIRST THING YOU SHOULD do if you are interested in Basic Underwater Demolition/SEAL (BUD/S) training is visit the official Navy SEAL website at http://www.sealswcc.com. Although my BUD/S experiences and the experiences of others have similarities to today's training regimen, BUD/S is constantly evolving, so it is critical to begin preparing at the official source. This will also ensure that you receive the most accurate and up-to-date information.

Familiarize

On the same website, at the top of the page are the following drop-down menus: **About**, **Become a SEAL**, **Training**, **Forum**, **Downloads**, and **Become a SWCC**. Although a perfect knowledge is not necessary, it's important to become familiar with the information under each of these drop-down menus.

Requirements

Within the **Become a SEAL** drop-down there are two columns—**Enlisted SEAL** or **SEAL Officer**. Under each of these, click on the **Requirements** link to see what is needed. For officer candidates, there is contact information if you have questions.

Enlisted vs. Officer

BUD/S accepts more enlisted men to training than officers. For those who do make it to training, not only do officers have to do what all the other trainees are doing, but they also have the added responsibility of leading their classes. (Senior enlisted men will share in this responsibility.) On top of that, SEAL instructors tend to demand more from officers academically (higher scores on written tests) than enlisted men. In other words, you'll have the best chance of making it to BUD/S—and through BUD/S—if you go the enlisted SEAL route. Once in the SEAL teams, enlisted men will also have more opportunities for deployment, specialized schools like sniper training, combat operations, and so on, than officers, who over the years become more and more involved in leadership/administrative duties.

On the other hand, it's important to keep in mind that most BUD/S trainees won't become SEALs, because of injuries through no fault of their own, dropping out, performance failures, or getting fired by the instructors. When these trainees are sent out to the navy fleet, the officers will receive better pay, more respect, and better living conditions than the enlisted men. Enlisted men are sent where the navy wants them, which can often mean chipping paint on a ship and swabbing decks, as I did for a while. (Over time, depending on the individual and the environment, these sailors may find opportunities to do jobs more in line with their personal interests and abilities.) If one chooses not to make the navy a career, officers will likely have better job prospects in the civilian world than enlisted sailors, particularly since officers have college degrees.

Some men choose a hybrid route of earning their degree before entering the navy and joining as an enlisted man. After becoming a SEAL, they deploy often with their platoon. Then upon getting most of their fill of being an enlisted SEAL, they have the option of applying to Officer Candidate School, where they have a chance to cross over to become SEAL officers. As new SEAL officers, they find their way back to a SEAL platoon and serve there, before moving on to duties outside the platoon that focus more on leadership/administrative responsibilities.

On the topic of college, you may attend a university and discover a greater passion for a specific subject than you have for becoming a SEAL. You may save yourself years and heartache by finding this out in college rather than in the navy, where you are bound by a four-year contract. So consider all your options carefully before you make your decision, and do what is right for you.

Application Steps

If you believe you can pass the requirements, click on **Application Steps** and follow the instructions carefully. For those wanting to become enlisted SEALs, choose one of three paths. Path one is for civilians, path two is for sailors in the navy, and path three is for transferring from another service. For **SEAL Officers**, under the column with the same name, choose the **Application Steps**.

Enlisted SEALs, Civilians

For civilians (path one), step one is to "Visit your local Navy Recruiter." As you complete this step, your recruiter should put you in touch with a SEAL Mentor. If your recruiter doesn't, ask your recruiter specifically when this will be done. If the recruiter can't explain this to your satisfaction, contact the SEAL Mentor directly by using the link at the end of step one, and your SEAL Mentor should be able to help you sort out problems with your recruiter. Of course, you should have already read the **Requirements** section (mentioned earlier), and if you clearly don't meet the requirements, you shouldn't waste the SEAL Mentor's time asking questions you already know the answers to.

Enlisted SEALs, Navy Sailors

If you're already in the navy, follow path two. Step one is to "Notify your Command" by submitting a Special Request

Chit. In step two, contact your career counselor and LPO or CPO. As with civilians, you should've already read the **Requirements** section (mentioned earlier). If you meet the requirements, step three is scheduling your physical screen test (PST). If you pass the PST, follow the remaining steps.

Enlisted SEALs, Transferring from Another Military Branch

If you're transferring from one of the other services (army, Marines, air force, Coast Guard), you have to wait until forty-five days before your enlistment contract is up before you can attempt a transfer. One young man told me that a Marine recruiter once told him, "Join the Marines, and you can transfer to become a SEAL." I tried to explain that he'd have to finish his enlistment with the Marines before he could take a shot at becoming a SEAL. My feeling is that if one's main goal is to become a SEAL, joining the navy is the most efficient route to achieving that goal. Unfortunately, some recruiters are more interested in filling quotas than helping prospective military men and women, so if you know what you want to do, do it.

Special Mission Units

If one's main goal is to become a special operator, the army, air force, and Marines also have special operations. At the tip of special operations are Special Mission Units (SMU).

As of this writing, the SMUs are the Navy's SEAL Team Six (a.k.a. DEVGRU), the army's Delta Force, and the air force's Combat Control Team (CCT) and Pararescue (PJ). Of course, the most common route in the navy to joining an SMU is first becoming a SEAL. In the army, the majority of SMU operators are former Rangers. Air force SMUs are taken from CCTs and PJs. The Marine Corps was the last to become a member of the US Special Operations Command, and as of this writing, Marines have not publicly been recognized as part of the Special Mission Units. When the Marine Corps does join the SMUs, these operators will most likely come from the Marine Corps Forces Special Operations Command (MARSOC). MARSOC has drawn most of its operators from Force Reconnaissance.

SEAL OFFICERS

In order to become a SEAL officer, candidates must first become commissioned from the US Naval Academy, Officer Candidate School (OCS), or the Naval Reserve Officer Training Corps (NROTC). On a limited basis, some officers are accepted to training from in-fleet transfers and other services, but the small number of officer slots are mostly given to the Naval Academy because they have the highest graduation rate at BUD/S and are in high demand. The remaining slots are mostly divided between OCS and NROTC. At the SEALs' official website, follow the appropriate link for the **Application Steps**.

Training

You must train in order to pass the physical screen test (PST) and be in the best possible condition for surviving BUD/S. On the official SEAL website, within the drop-down menu for **Training** is a **Physical Prep** column. Here you'll find the *NSW PT Guide*, which is particularly helpful for preparing. Some guys think they have to lift a lot of weights and bulk up to get through BUD/S, but they don't understand that having muscular endurance, similar to that of a triathlete, is more important than becoming a power lifter or looking like Dwayne "the Rock" Johnson. Under this same column, it's also useful to study the info on **Swimming**, **Running**, **Strength**, **Injury Prevention**, and **Nutrition**.

To the right of the **Physical Prep** column, the heading says **Mental Prep**, but underneath here you can click the link to **SEAL Videos** and find more about training. For example, the swim video will help show you how to swim faster. The nutrition video talks about the waste of money and potential harm in buying supplements, which are not allowed in training—you only need a thousand milligrams of calcium (three glasses of milk) and a thousand milligrams of vitamin C (a glass of orange juice and some fruit) a day, in addition to a balanced diet. Supplements beyond this are banned in training and will get you in trouble.

In my case, I'd taken unnecessary megavitamins before training—much more than I needed. I hadn't realized I was putting extra strain on my body because I had to piss out a lot of extra junk. Fortunately, when I showed up at BUD/S, the instructors told us to get rid of all that supplement crap, and we followed their advice, leading to positive results.

You'll be rewarded by training effectively rather than underpreparing, overpreparing, or improperly preparing. These are the critical building blocks to beginning SEAL training. As you master these building blocks, your strength of belief will increase.

FAQs

At the top of the official SEAL website, under the **Become a SEAL** drop-down menu, there are two categories where frequently asked questions (FAQ) appear: **Enlisted SEALs** and **SEAL Officer**. A number of common questions are answered under both categories.

Forums

There are two official forums on the SEAL website at the time of this writing. One is under the **Become a SEAL** drop-down menu, under the **SEAL Officer** column—**SEAL Officer forum**. The other is one of the headings at the top of the drop-down menu—**Forum**. You'll find useful information in both places, but it's important to keep in mind that some of these discussions can stray into areas that can be confusing for a beginner. When that happens, just return to the official SEAL website and focus on mastering the basics.

Use Your Resources

There is a lot of information available from a variety of sources, but the most accurate and up-to-date information is available free on the official SEAL website: http://www.sealswcc.com. Master this before investing time (and money) and chasing your tail on other advice that may or may not be helpful. If you can begin following the advice from active-duty SEAL instructors and active-duty SEAL cadre now, it'll be easier to follow their advice later, and you'll be closer to your goal.

Good luck!

References

Bosiljevac, T. L. *SEALs: UDT/SEAL Operations in Vietnam.* Boulder, Colorado: Paladin Press, 1990.

Couch, Dick. *The Warrior Elite: The Forging of SEAL Class 228.* New York: Three Rivers Press, 2001.

Coulson, Danny O., and Elaine Shannon. *No Heroes: Inside the FBI's Secret Counter-Terror Force.* New York: Pocket Books, 1999.

Norris, Thomas. "Medal of Honor Series: Thomas Norris," Pritzker Military Library. January 29, 2009. http://www.pritzkermilitarylibrary.org/events/2009/01-29-thomas-norris.jsp (accessed September 20, 2010).

Norris, Thomas, and Michael Thornton. "Medal of Honor Series: Thomas Norris and Michael Thornton." Pritzker Military Library. November 9, 2006. http://www.pritzkermilitarylibrary.org/events/2006/11-09-thornton-norris.jsp (accessed September 20, 2010).

Wasdin, Howard, and Stephen Templin. *SEAL Team Six: Memoirs of an Elite Navy SEAL Sniper.* New York: St. Martin's Press, 2011.

Acknowledgments

THANKS TO C. FOR TAKING time after Hell Week to update me on the knots for underwater knot tying—any errors are my own. I greatly appreciate Danielle Poiesz for her editorial advice on an earlier draft of this book. Most of all, I am thankful for the support of my wife, Reiko, and my children, Kent and Maria.

An excerpt from

Trident's First Gleaming

A Special Operations Group Thriller
Stephen Templin

CHAPTER 1

Fall 2009

CHRIS PALADIN SPED THROUGH THE murky straightaway, the foul, viscid air of the Euphrates clogging his nostrils. The camouflage he and the other six SEALs wore couldn't hide them from the rank wind when going nearly forty knots against the dying flow of the ancient river. Around them, the desert choked the stretches of the bank, leaving the land barren as they raced into Syria.

Chris glanced at Little Doc sitting next to him.

Only weeks ago, back at their base in Al Anbar Province, Iraq, Chris and Little Doc had paired off in a game of pool against a talented Agency cyber warfare tech named Young Park and a top spook, Hannah Andrade. They'd played an epic contest of SEALs versus CIA. But so much had changed since then.

Young's kidnapping was why they were out here now. Those damn tangos had dressed up as Iraqi troops while Chris and his crew were out on an op and snatched the man.

And along with him, potentially dangerous knowledge that needed kept out of enemy hands.

A terrorist named Professor Mordet was behind it all, intelligence told them. Chris struggled to focus on the mission rather than his anger. This mission was personal—and a top priority for JSOC and the Agency. He had to keep a clear head.

He took a breath and pushed back the messy emotions, locking them down in the depths of his psyche. His laser focus picked apart the dark fig palms and tangles of weeds that appeared on the port side shore. He searched for anyone or anything that might deny their rescue.

After traveling another klick, off the starboard side became farmland, too, dotted with a scattering of farmhouses. Where there were buildings, there were people, and Chris didn't want to meet any of them. He only wanted to see two people, the kidnapper and the hostage.

Even when there weren't farmhouses, there might be people, he reminded himself. *Expect the unexpected.*

Chris surveyed his team. They carried light, sound-suppressed weapons, and to add to their stealth and speed, they'd dispensed with their bullet-resistant vests. The moonlight negated much of the advantage of night vision goggles, too, so they'd left the cumbersome devices behind. Although some might consider going without reckless, it was one of many tactics they'd used with monster success again and again. They were ready.

Several more klicks up the river, a shadowy island emerged in the middle of the Euphrates, and the coxswain veered to the starboard side, putting the Special Operations Craft–Riverine (SOC-R) in a stretch that cut the river's width in half. On each side of their boat, there were only fifty meters between the frogmen and the shore—close enough for enemy assault rifles and machine guns to tear into them. Chris and his team continued to scan 360 degrees around their boat.

If the enemy is expecting us, this would be the place to stick it to us.

Chris's pulse quickened at the thought. In Basic Underwater Demolition/SEAL (BUD/S) training, he'd learned to control his fear by remembering a peaceful experience, like when he was a child riding his bicycle, but after repeated practice, he could skip the remembering and trigger the result by using one word: *breathe*.

He took a deep breath and exhaled. His pulse slowed.

Breathe.

Then his pulse crawled.

Anyone who says they aren't scared is a liar or an idiot.

Chris and the guys on the port side of the SOC-R studied the vegetation, looking for movement or the sudden flash of an enemy AK-47 muzzle. The SEALs on the starboard side did the same. The boat passed the small island, then another. After half a klick, the SOC-R slowed, pulled up against the mainland bank on the port side, and stopped.

They hopped over the side of the boat and onto land. The bulkiest SEAL, nicknamed Beanpole as a joke, slipped on the muddy bank but caught himself, narrowly preventing a noisy back flop into the water. Chris scowled. Beanpole was a joke. He told the officers and senior enlisted men what they wanted to hear and told them often, but in the field, he was a tactical loser. Two weeks earlier, Chris's squad had lost a teammate during an ambush. Chris and the others had mourned his loss. Although eager to add another gun to their side, they were disappointed to find out that the new gun was Beanpole.

The olive-drab-colored SEALs faded into the vegetation, then crouched while the navy SOC-R crew sped upriver to do a couple false insertions in order to confuse anyone who might be paying attention. Chris and his teammates crouched, waited, and listened for surprise guests. Although the SEALs had inserted as silently as ninjas, the unknown was still out there, and it could sneak up at any time and stab him in the back. Running ops every night for as long as he had, and multiple times in the same night, he'd snatched or killed more tangos than he could remember, but the one fact that had been seared into his mind was that the hunter could always become the hunted.

A strange darkness permeated the area, despite the moonlight. Chris tried to pinpoint the reason for the blackness, but even where the moon shone, gloom remained, as if each particle of plants and dirt rejected the sky's illumination. There were no clouds or any indication of a storm front arriving. Yet a dark, giant hand seemed to press down on him.

After fifteen minutes of lying low, adrenaline was pumping freely through his veins, heightening his senses and making him stronger. Chris's patrol leader, a senior chief, signaled for them to move out. Then the point man, nicknamed Gorgeous because hordes of women wanted to have his babies, led the SEALs out, and Psycho brought up the rear. In the middle, Chris and the others watched everything to the left and right of their crew.

The SEALs eased out of the dense vegetation and walked into a winter wheat field. After they patrolled 150 meters, the field came to an end, and the men lay prone on the hard ground. Even though the wheat protected them from prying eyes, it wouldn't protect them from bullets. Chris peeked through the wheat. Fifty meters ahead stood their target building—the back of a two-story structure with an expansive roof. Each floor had thin, white wooden columns along it, thirty-meter wide porches, and French doors. The French colonial plantation house seemed eerily surreal sitting on the Syrian landscape, where humble farmhouses sat on small plots of land to the south.

The silhouette of a guard was visible, ghostlike, on a large wooden chair on the left side of the first-floor porch. An AK-47 stood propped between his legs. Hannah's asset had reported that one guard always sat on the porch in front of the house, but Chris couldn't see that one yet. Another guard was supposed to be inside. Chris didn't want to shoot Ghost from their current position and risk hitting a window and waking up the neighborhood.

He signaled for Psycho to follow him, and the two stalked from their six o'clock position clockwise using hibiscus shrubs for cover until they reached nine o'clock, the edge of the porch, ten meters away from Ghost.

Chris peered into his sight, where a red dot floated in the middle without projecting out for others to see. He aligned the red dot on the side of Ghost's head and squeezed the trigger, then rapidly aligned and squeezed again: *phht*, *phht*. The guard's upper body flopped sideways over the chair's armrest with the AK-47 still between his legs. Chris's heart smiled at the satisfaction of completing his task, and his pulse calmed with the relief that he'd taken out a potential threat.

Chris wasn't born a killer; he valued life as much as most people in the human family. As a child, he'd once killed a bird with a BB gun. His stomach had revolted at what he'd done, and he never did it again. But also as a child, the son of US diplomats in Syria, terrorists had kidnapped him and killed a classmate; as a result, Chris considered terrorists to be disposable members of his species. The tragic deaths of 9/11 had reinforced his distaste for terrorists and spurred him to join the military. Drawing on similar strengths that helped him survive his kidnapping, he'd survived SEAL training, and it was during that training that he'd further dehumanized the enemy by focusing on their crimes against humanity and shooting them in the form of paper and steel targets. The first time he'd killed a real terrorist, his stomach had churned and he'd become somewhat light-headed, but the more he'd killed, the more that feeling had gone away until he no longer had the feeling. Although he could remember the mud huts, dusty alley, and body of the first man he'd killed, he couldn't remember the name of the village or the man's face. He remembered the sick feeling of taking a life but not the mission—when it came to fighting, either the enemy died or Chris died. Even worse, if he didn't do his job, his teammates could get hurt.

Chris wouldn't let that happen. The tango was a threat, and then he wasn't.

One down.

Chris had eliminated so many insurgents since then that he couldn't count them all, and in his memory, they faded into a blur. Most SEAL ops were considered perfect if no shooting occurred, but he and his crew hardly lived in a perfect world. Now they had to find Young, and the danger zone was about to heat up.

Chris and Psycho sneaked around to the front, and Psycho dispatched another guard. Chris keyed the transmitter on his radio once, signaling the others to advance to the back door. The sentry removal duo returned to the back door, and Chris tried to open it—no luck. He looked at the lock—the keyhole was upside down from American locks. He inserted the small length of an L-shaped Quiet Steel tension wrench into the top of the keyhole and turned it. Then he took a Quiet Steel pick, a long, thin bar with a hook at the end, and poked it into the bottom of the keyhole until it reached the back of the lock. He finessed them until the door unlocked.

Chris opened the door, and the others poured in first. Chris brought up the rear as he stepped into a well-furnished room. There were two doorways, so their crew split up into two teams, and Chris's slipped into a living room lit by the moonlight through the French windows. He turned left, staying close to the wall. From the couch stood a guard with an AK in his hand. He raised the muzzle in Chris's direction. Chris fired twice into his chest—*phht, phht*—then once in his head—*phht*—dropping him to the floor. Between training and real experiences, he'd done this thousands of times, and his motor skills functioned with an automaticity like breathing.

After both fire teams cleared the first deck, they crept up an unlit stairway to the second deck. The first fire team approached the door on the left, and Chris's team moved to the door on the right. Now, the giant black hand that had been pressing on him since they'd set foot on the grounds pressed harder, as if to bury him under heaven and earth.

Something ungodly is behind that door.

His pulse quickened, and he lost control of his speeding respiration as he turned the knob—locked.

It was a simple lock, so Chris simply slid his pick in and gently turned it. A thump sounded against the wall—Chris's heart rate launched into hyperdrive—and he glanced at his team. Beanpole's muzzle swayed in his hands. He must've tapped the wall. Chris and others gave Beanpole a dirty look.

The door unlocked and Chris pushed it open. Beanpole and Psycho entered first. Chris followed. His gaze darted around the room. A man lay still on a silky bed sheet, unmoving. Professor Mordet, the kidnapper. And next to the bed was an empty bottle of wine. He'd played right into the SEALs' hands; he was out cold.

Chris and Psycho zip-tied Mordet's hands behind his back while Beanpole duct-taped his mouth. When Chris and Psycho had finished the zip ties, Beanpole was already putting a black hood over Mordet's head.

The three SEALs poked and prodded Mordet until he awoke. He fought to free himself and scream, but Psycho struck him down. When he regained consciousness, they helped him to his feet. Now he was compliant.

They left the room and slammed him to the floor in the hall before propping him up on his knees.

Chris and Psycho helped quickly clear the other rooms while Beanpole stayed with Mordet.

After clearing each room, they scoured the house for hidden rooms or other areas where Mordet might be keeping Young. The SEALs bagged intel: USB sticks, DVDs, laptops, papers, and other items. There was no sign of Young in the building, diffusing Chris's hopes of rescuing him tonight.

Chris kicked the wall, making a hole. "Shit!"

Back in the hall, Beanpole continued to guard Mordet, who sat with a meditative stillness.

Gorgeous led them out of the house with the same hushed discipline they'd had as they'd arrived. They headed toward the river. On the return trip was when it was natural to sigh a breath of relief, but for Chris, the pucker factor was higher.

This is the time when men make mistakes; this is the time when men get killed.

Mordet fell.

Did he really fall, or is he trying to slow us down on purpose?

Beanpole jerked him to his feet.

The squad didn't use the same route they'd taken when they'd arrived, in case someone had seen their insertion and was waiting to spring an ambush on them. They slipped into a neighboring field with its wheat tips stabbing at the sky like arrowheads. The SEALs patrolled to the end of the field, heading for their haven—the water. Just before they exited the wheat field, the guys in front of Chris dropped to the ground and stayed there. Chris lowered himself to the prone position, too. He glanced behind—Beanpole pushed Mordet into the dirt, and Beanpole and Psycho lay low. Soon, Little Doc gave Chris the hand signal: *enemy ahead*. Chris relayed the message behind.

Even if there was only one insurgent, he might be the point man for a whole squad, platoon, or battalion of insurgents. With only one SOC-R sitting hidden upstream and no airpower on site for support, the SEALs were probably outgunned. They'd bagged their man, and now wasn't the time to become greedy—and end up in a body bag. They had to stay still.

I am the earth, Chris thought to himself. *I am the ground.* He relaxed all his muscles, sinking deeper to become one with the ground. *I am the earth*, he repeated to himself. *I am the earth.* His heart rate and breathing slowed to an almost vegetative state.

The sound of men's voices and footsteps came from the direction of the river. Maybe two squads. The insurgents were home now and obviously feeling relaxed and secure—talking loudly. As they neared the SEALs, their voices and footsteps became more and more careless. The insurgent point man came so close to Chris that he could have reached out and grabbed him. The insurgent passed.

As Chris lay flat on the ground holding his MP7 in both hands, he waited for the other insurgents to go by. Something rustled on the ground followed by a scream for help in Arabic. Before Chris could react, a shadow leaped onto his back, and something clamped down on his ear and caused a sharp pain, like a wild animal biting him—*Mordet*! Chris wanted to leap and cry out, but he gulped down his fear and pain. With his right hand still holding the MP7, he reached around with his left hand, found Mordet's face, and drove his thumb between the man's nose and eyeball, popping the eye out of its socket. Mordet wouldn't let go as he chewed off half of Chris's ear. White heat traveled from Chris's ear, through his body, and to the tips of his right toes—sapping the strength out of him. Mordet had the strength of a mad goblin. Chris's world became pale as he tried to stop his attacker. He was passing out.

A crack sounded, and Mordet's head bumped against Chris's. The goblin gave up gobbling. Chris turned his head to find Mordet unconscious and Little Doc pulling the butt of his MP7 away from Mordet's noggin. Mordet was lucky. Little Doc had only struck him with the butt and hadn't shot him—they still needed to interrogate the beast in order to find Young.

The duct tape and eye were hanging from Mordet's face, and his black hood lay on the ground next to him. He'd probably fallen on his face multiple times to loosen the tape. The zip ties had proven to be tougher, though, and Mordet's hands were still bound. Little Doc calmly put Mordet's eye back in.

The other SEALs fired their sound-suppressed MP7s, which emitted no flash, at the two squads. Chris faced inland and saw enemy muzzles flashing from multiple directions. The insurgents could hear the SEALs but couldn't see them. With the red dot in Chris's sight, he traced one muzzle flash to the upper body of a long silhouette. Chris squeezed his trigger once. Then again. The long silhouette sank.

Although the insurgents fired their AKs on full auto, the SEAL squad's precise shots severed the tangos' numbers—until the fight became mano a mano. Untamed power surged through Chris's veins, and he felt like a wolf with his wolf pack, dominating the night.

The surviving tangos wised up—AK muzzle flashes focused on the SEALs' direction, and mini sonic booms from passing bullets popped the air around him. He efficiently took the fear of the bullets and locked it into a tiny box. He had entered a zone, focusing even more on his next target. Chris eased his red dot on the nearest insurgent and downed him. The insurgent's comrades fell, too—until none were left standing.

If the insurgents had been the target of this mission, Chris and his teammates would check to make sure they were all dead and search them for intel, but they weren't the target, and a few hundred Syrian militiamen from Mordet's village were probably en route to the frogmen's position right now.

After making so much noise, there was no more need for stealth. Senior Chief barked, "Haul ass to the river!"

Chris picked the black hood off the ground and turned to make sure Beanpole and Psycho were following. Beanpole poked Mordet in the back, and he stumbled forward.

As they ran to the river, blood oozed from Chris's bitten ear and down his neck. He didn't know how much blood he'd lost, but there was no time to bandage himself now. When the SEALs reached the water, the SOC-R was waiting for them with its engines running. They boarded swiftly and took their designated positions. The pilot shoved the throttle forward, and the boat pulled away from the bank and accelerated to over forty knots, heading south.

"Status report," Senior called to the SEALs.

Gorgeous sounded off first, reporting on any wounds and remaining ammo: "Gorgeous, okay, four magazines." The others sounded off in succession. Then came Chris's turn. "Reverend, got a nick on my right ear, three magazines." "Reverend" was Chris's call sign—given to him because when the guys went barhopping, despite relentless ribbing, Chris wouldn't drink alcohol. Psycho gave the last report.

Beanpole made eye contact with Chris for a moment. Chris was pissed.

If you'd gagged Mordet properly, this wouldn't have happened.

Beanpole looked away as if he could read his thoughts.

Little Doc came over to take a look at his ear while the guys with more ammo donated bullets to the guys with less.

As Little Doc examined Chris, he calmly said, "Looks like they shot off half of your ear. Did you pick it up and bring it with you?"

Mordet had a grin on his face as he chewed on something. Chris pointed to him and said, "He bit it off."

"What?" Little Doc asked.

Mordet continued to chew.

Disgust and anger roiled in Chris's stomach. "What the—damn, he's eating it!"

"Eat this!" Little Doc slammed the butt of his rifle into Mordet's face. The chewing motion stopped. Little Doc grabbed Mordet's nose with one hand and his jaw with the other and opened Mordet's mouth wide. "You sicko-freako-shit-sucking-no-life-mother—" He shook half of a chewed-up ear out of Mordet's mouth. It was impractical for them to carry ice in the field, so Little Doc wrapped the piece of flesh in some gauze and put it in Chris's shirt pocket.

They sat silently until Mordet regained consciousness. This time, Little Doc struck him so hard with the rifle butt that it probably knocked his IQ down twenty points. Little Doc gagged him again before Chris slammed the hood down around Mordet's head.

As the SEALs continued their return trip, Little Doc disinfected and bandaged Chris's ear.

Will my ear ever be the same again? I hope I don't bleed to death.

His enlistment was near its end, and this wasn't giving him warm, fuzzy feelings about re-upping. Then he realized that if he kept thinking about his ear and reenlistment, he might miss spotting an ambush and lose more than his ear. He focused his eyes and mind on the shore, scanning for threats.

The SEALs traveled unmolested to their base in Al Anbar Province, where they handed Mordet over to the civilian-clothed Agency interrogator and his assistants.

A hospital corpsman showed up soon after and escorted Chris away.

In sick bay, the surgeon greeted Chris, who took his piece of ear out of his pocket.

The surgeon didn't have to examine it long to make a judgment: "This is too mangled. Even if I did sew it back on, it would remain deformed like this for the rest of your life."

"Right now, all I want to do is find Young."

"After I sew up your wound here, I can arrange to have you flown to the facial prosthetics lab at Lackland Air Force Base in San Antonio. Their 3-D camera can produce images for a mold of your ear. I can even arrange for you to have a summer ear and winter ear with appropriate skin tones and an ear in camouflage."

"Thanks, Doc, but I don't have time right now to fly back to the States. That'll have to wait until after we find Young."

"I'll just sew it up for now."

Chris nodded.

As the surgeon went to work, Chris noticed his Yale diploma on the wall and remembered his sophomore year at

Harvard. At that time, part of Chris had wanted to become a preacher and part of him had wanted to become a SEAL, but when 9/11 happened, the choice had become clear: he'd left Harvard and joined the navy. Now he hunted evil men through fire and brimstone, and although he repeatedly reminded himself that he wasn't a part of the bad guys' underworld, he bore the scars of their world on his body and soul. He longed for light. He longed for a place closer to heaven.

After the surgeon finished suturing his wound, Chris departed and hurried to the gator pit, where he found Hannah watching a live video feed of the interrogation. She was a raven-haired chameleon who shape-shifted between geek, Sampson, and Delilah.

Hannah's eyes didn't leave the video feed as Chris stepped up beside her. "What's a nice guy like you doing in a place like this?" she asked with a sweetness in her husky voice.

He smiled. "Same thing a nice gal like you is doing." He pointed to the monitor. "What is he doing?"

"Waterboarding Mordet," she said.

"And?" Chris asked.

"Mordet hasn't said a word."

The interrogation booth was a small room made of plywood. A TV monitor on the wall was hooked up to a laptop on a table, so if Mordet began talking about Young's location, the gator could have Mordet point it out on a high-tech map on the TV monitor. Mordet was tied on his back on a board the size of a door, with his feet elevated. A wet orange cloth was wrapped around his face.

The gator's head looked like a lemon—it had more width than height, and his skin color was jaundiced. He also had the muscle mass of a bodybuilder. Gator nodded to his assistant, who poured a gallon water jug from two feet above Mordet's nose and mouth. Immediately, Mordet gagged. Seconds later, his body went limp. Either he was too tired to fight or he was purposely allowing his nose and mouth to fill up with water and causing himself to asphyxiate. The average person would begin talking by fifteen seconds—saying anything, truth or lies, to make the waterboarding stop. Each session would last no longer than forty seconds but could be repeated for up to twelve minutes in a day.

"How long have they been doing this?" Chris asked.

"About half an hour," she said matter-of-factly.

"I'm not complaining, but does Lemon Head know what he's doing?"

Hannah shrugged. "He's a contractor."

"We really don't have time for amateur hour. Young doesn't have time." Chris left the gator pit and rushed to the interrogation booth, where he burst inside the cramped room.

Gator turned around, and his brow furrowed. "What the hell?"

Mordet stirred as if from a sleep. Water trickled from his nose and mouth.

Chris motioned for Gator to step out of the room with him. The man gestured to his assistant to watch their prisoner.

They exited the booth and walked down the hall. "I was in the middle of an interrogation," Gator said.

"The middle?" Chris asked.

Gator puffed out his chest. "I'll break him," he said proudly.

"I can see that." Chris was unable to hide the sarcasm in his voice.

"Who are you?"

"We can't launch a rescue until we know where Young is."

Gator came to a stop in the pit near where Hannah sat. "Tell me something I don't know."

"Young is running out of time and—"

"You can't rush progress," Gator interrupted.

Chris stared hard at him, and tension filled his voice. "We're out of time."

Gator leaned forward. "My interrogation was working until you interrupted."

Chris stood his ground. "Maybe you can update me on the intel you already extracted."

With his index finger, Gator poked Chris in the chest. "You need to chill."

"I am chill." Chris pushed the finger away from his chest.

"You don't seem chill to me."

"Maybe I can persuade Mordet to talk."

Gator leaned in even closer so Chris could feel the heat and smell the bunghole-stink of his breath. "Maybe you don't understand who's in charge here."

"I'm not asking to take over," Chris said. "You can take credit for any intel I acquire. I'm just asking for a shot at Mordet."

"You hot-shits think you can do anything you want because everyone's scared of you. Well, I'm not scared of you."

"I'm not trying to scare you. I just want to find Young."

"So does everyone else, but I'm the one who knows about interrogation, and you need to get authorization before you interrogate the prisoner!"

"Are you saying you have no authority here?"

"I have authority!"

Chris tried to remain calm. "I only know that I was waterboarded in SERE school. And I've worked with some of the best gators in the business. And you're not one of them."

Hannah, still sitting in her chair in front of the live video monitor, chuckled.

Chris turned to her and said, "Tell those guys in the booth to stop screwing around and prepare the prisoner for interrogation."

She left the pit and headed to the booth.

"You can't do this," Gator said.

Chris moved in so close that he was toe to toe with Gator. "Saving Young is *deadly* important to me," Chris said quietly. "How important is it to you?"

The veins in Gator's neck bulged as if they were about to pop.

Chris prepared to flip his inner switch from chill to bone-burning conflagration.

"Your commanding officer will hear about this!"

Chris didn't know whether Gator was smart for not fighting or cowardly for backing off. Maybe he was both. "I'm sure he will."

Gator kicked a trash bucket across the room on his way out.

"Does anyone know where I can get a good bottle of wine ASAP?" Chris shouted out to the others in the gator pit.

A man in civilian clothes hesitantly raised his hand.

"I need it for the interrogation. How fast can you get it here?" Chris asked.

"Right away." The man left his desk and rushed out of the room.

"If Mordet likes wine and my ear, I'll give him what he wants." Chris borrowed Hannah's phone, called the surgeon, and asked for his ear in a small cooler.

He observed the monitor of the interrogation booth. Gator's henchman cleared out the waterboarding equipment, handcuffed Mordet's hands behind his back, chained his feet together, and sat him in a chair.

Minutes later, when the cooler and wine arrived, Chris left the gator pit. After the henchman stepped out of the booth, Chris stepped inside. He closed the door behind him and set his cooler down beside the door. Then he took a seat on the plastic chair in front of a table between himself and Mordet.

It's time we have a little chat, my friend.

CHAPTER 2

THE BOOTH, LIKE OTHER INTERROGATION rooms, was kept cold to make the prisoner uncomfortable. Chris exhaled, purging any anger or anxiety from his system—neither would help him succeed in the interrogation.

Mordet gazed at the bandage on Chris's ear. "I gather that we have already made each other's acquaintance, but my doctorate is in philosophy, not medicine."

Chris felt the same giant, dark hand pressing down on him that he'd experienced at Mordet's estate. "You gather correctly, Professor." Chris poured a glass of wine and gave him a sip.

After Mordet finished the sip, he licked his lips. "It seems that you know about me, but I do not know about you, other than the fact that you and your comrades were highly professional, and we left via the Euphrates River. No conventional military units would operate inside Syria. I can only guess that you are a Navy SEAL—probably from SEAL Team Six." Mordet stared into Chris's eyes as if he were probing Chris's brain.

Chris showed no expression in his face or voice. "I can neither confirm nor deny—"

Mordet was equally cool. "No need—I have already confirmed it. Even so, I still do not know your name."

Chris didn't know how the interrogation would play out, but if he was patient, he might spot an opening and exploit it. "My name is Chris."

Mordet's eyes sparkled. "Do you have a last name, Chris?"

Chris continued without showing emotion. "Yes."

Mordet took another drink. "Will you give it to me?"

"No."

The sparkle in Mordet's eyes faded. "That is not very sporting. You have come here to ask me where Young Park is, but you will not even tell me your last name."

"Yes, I came here to ask where he is." Chris gave him the rest of the drink.

He seemed pleased. "Why is he so important to you?"

Chris refilled Mordet's glass. He had thought he was in control of the interrogation, but now he wasn't sure. He gave Mordet a long drink.

"Is Park related to you?"

Chris said nothing.

"A friend?"

"Yes."

Mordet stared at Chris's eyes. "This rescue has more meaning to you than mere friendship. Maybe this is more about the rescue than about Young Park."

The remarks caught Chris off guard, as if Mordet had a sixth sense for digging into his soul. Every rescue was deeply personal, but the purpose of the interrogation was Young, not Chris. He surveyed for a warm spot in Mordet's cool veneer. "You bit off my ear and tried to eat it. Don't you think that's a bit strange?"

Mordet gazed at the ceiling. "Is it? During the Vietnam War, a CIA SOG officer killed enemy combatants and cut off their ears. And made necklaces out of them." Mordet sniffed the air as if he smelled a meal, and then his eyes lowered to his interrogator.

Mordet had an aura about him that made Chris's skin prickle, but he didn't show it. "I've heard the stories. I've heard a lot of stories and seen a lot of things, but you weren't making a necklace."

Mordet frowned like a lecturer disappointed with a student. "What would be the point—a trophy? How droll. And wasteful."

"I don't know anyone who eats the body parts of humans."

There was a shadowy stillness in Mordet's eyes, and wine stained the corner of his lips like blood. "In western New Guinea, when the Korowai tribe finds that someone is a *khakhua*, a witch doctor, they eat that person's brain while it is still warm."

Chris saw the source of the giant, dark hand that pressed on him, and the more he saw, the less he wanted to see, but he didn't show his aversion to the blackness emanating from Mordet. "I didn't know that," he said matter-of-factly.

Mordet smiled, but the corners of his smile were closer to a sneer. "In America, when the Donner Party became trapped in the snowy Sierra Nevada, the survivors ate the dead."

"That remains unconfirmed."

"In the 1972 Andes flight disaster, the survivors ate the dead bodies of their classmates and friends."

Mordet disgusted Chris, and the conversation made him weary, much like the war did, but Mordet gave off an aura of evil unlike any Chris had ever encountered. In spite of his weariness and his need to end the conversation, his need to rescue Young was greater.

What makes you tick, Mordet?

"But I don't guess you belong to a tribe in New Guinea nor were you in the Andes flight disaster."

"Not the Andes flight disaster, but when I was a teenager, my mother, younger sister, and I flew to Turkey for a winter vacation. We crashed in the Taurus Mountains. Only my sister and I survived. After we ran out of food, I suggested we eat the bodies. My sister refused and insisted we try to climb off the mountain. I told her the weather was too severe and it would be easier for a search party to find a wrecked plane than two people wandering through the snow. So I did what was necessary to survive, but I will never forget the way she looked at me, like I was . . . such a monster. Two days later, I woke up and she was gone. One month after the crash, they rescued me and found my sister's body. She'd frozen to death." He finished his drink.

"You ate human flesh for nourishment." Chris refilled his glass and gave him a drink.

"Yes, of course. When I returned home, news traveled about how I'd survived, and my classmates and their parents ostracized me. Sometimes I fantasized about eating them. I read about the Korowai tribe and was fascinated. Of course eating another human is part of their culture, but more important, eating another human gives them spiritual power to destroy forces greater than mortality."

"But eating my ear didn't give you the power to escape. You're still imprisoned here."

"Ah, but I did not finish the whole ear, you see."

Chris wanted to put a bullet through him, but he exercised patience instead. "I'm not here to judge you. I just want to know where Young is."

"Why should I help you?" Mordet looked at the cooler and bottle of wine near the doorway. "If you give me a bottle of wine and what is left of your ear in that cooler, you think I'll tell you where Young is?"

Mordet's weakness seemed to be his pride in his intellect and his eagerness to rationalize his cannibalism as some mystic gift. "You suggested that if you could finish the ear, your spiritual power would increase, enabling you to escape this situation." Chris moved his chair closer to Mordet. "Jeffrey Dahmer ate people because his brain was a couple bullets short of a full magazine. I'm just trying to confirm how I should classify our conversation in the report I send to my superiors and our allies."

Chris gave him the rest of the glass, but he didn't pour a refill. "*Très bien*. I am not so strange. If you had walked in my shoes, you would have done the same." Mordet whispered: "During my senior year of high school—"

"If you're not interested, I understand." Chris stood up, turned around, and walked to the door. He picked up his cooler. "I think I know how to write my report."

"Wait," Mordet said.

Chris stopped and turned to face him.

"Give me the wine and cooler, and I will tell you where Young is."

"It doesn't work that way. After we find Young, you get what's left of the wine and my ear. I'll write a report about your belief in your mystic power. Then it's up to you to prove to everyone that your power is real. Now, if you'll excuse me, I have work to do." Chris reached for the door.

"Patience, patience. I will tell you where he is."

Chris anxiously fingered the lighter in his pocket. "You can tell the interrogator. If your information helps us rescue Young, you get the wine and my ear. And I'll update my report. Until then, talk is cheap."

"This rescue means more to you than Young himself. Why is the rescue so important to you?"

His own kidnapping flashed back to him. The feelings of despair, of terror. The darkness of the pit he'd been kept in. The aftermath.

"Good-bye, Professor."

"Will you leave me your e-mail address in case I think of something more?"

Chris walked out the door without turning back. He wanted to run, putting as much distance between himself and Mordet as he could, but he denied Mordet his influence and walked at a normal pace. He wanted to teleport himself out of this hell—far from the despots and devils. Events after that were a spinning blur to him. He didn't know if it was the exhaustion of the op, blood loss from his ear, or the soul-sucking interrogation that drained him, but somehow he found his way to his rack and lay down.

Just over an hour later, Little Doc came to Chris's rack. "Come on! We're going to get Young!"

They geared up with their teammates and rushed across the gray tarmac to where two Black Hawks and a smaller Little Bird MH-6 helicopter were already spinning up. His adrenaline beat with the *thwop-thwop* of the choppers' blades. The helos were waiting for Chris, LT, and his seven men.

Hannah met Chris partway and shouted above the noise. "The gator took the credit, but it was because of you that Mordet gave us Young's location!" There was a twinkle in her eyes that he'd only seen when they'd first met, and it made his soul soar.

"No, we found Mordet because of you and your asset!" He wanted to hug her—and he wanted to be finished with the war on terror—but now he had to find Young. Everything else would just have to wait.

"We'll play pool when you get back!" she said.

He nodded. Hannah was a talented colleague and a good friend, and in moments like this, he wanted to get to know her better. It seemed like the time to say something epic, but all that came out of his mouth were two words: "Thank you!" He turned and sprinted to the chopper without looking back.

The helos were painted a dark green, but in the night, they loomed black. Their blades beat the air with a *thwop-thwop-thwop*, making the earth quiver beneath Chris's feet as he neared his Black Hawk. Their rhythm continued to pulse in his blood. He took a seat inside with Senior Chief and their squad. LT and his squad of seven SEALs boarded the other Black Hawk. Two snipers, one starboard and one port, sat on the Little Bird with their legs dangling outside the helo. Diesel fumes struck Chris's sinuses like holy incense.

This time, instead of carrying the smaller sound-suppressed MP7 nine-millimeter submachine guns, Chris and his mates carried the more powerful HK416 5.56 assault rifles, wore bullet-resistant vests, and carried a deadly assortment of grenades. Every available pocket bulged with extra ammo. This was not a stealth mission.

The helos slowly lifted off the tarmac. Clouds blanketed the sky and the world shone green and 2-D from underneath his night vision goggles. One of the snipers flipped his middle finger at Chris's helo. Chris grinned and returned the greeting.

Soon they picked up speed, and the blades' *thwop-thwop-thwop* was drowned out by the roaring wind. The three helos hugged the earth so close and traveled so fast that it looked like the ground would tear off the Black Hawks' skids. The choppers raced northwest along a dry riverbed before speeding north through a valley. They dodged and hurdled sand dunes, houses, power lines, and palm trees before crossing the Syrian border.

Mordet's men were keeping Young in a dried-up well. Chris knew the tactic all too well. While his parents worked at the US embassy in Syria, he had been kidnapped and held for four days in a dried-up well outside of town, eventually rescued by SEALs. A shiver ran through him, and he tried to push the memory away.

The helos continued forward, then flew up at a steep angle, clearing a cluster of two-story buildings. Then the birds dived at the earth like kamikaze planes. At the last moment, their beaks flared up, halting the birds before leveling above an empty field near Mordet's plantation. Chris and his teammates quickly stepped onto the skids, then hopped down into a field surrounded by a cloud of dust kicked up by the helos.

The two squads moved at double time. The fourteen SEALs swiftly reached their objective, the well. Two armed Syrians emerged from a lopsided farmhouse—only to be picked off by the snipers hovering in the Little Bird above.

Chris looked down into the well with an overwhelming sense of déjà vu. Suddenly he was a thirteen-year-old boy trapped in that well again. He struggled to breathe. His chest tightened.

Breathe, Chris. Breathe.

But he still wasn't getting enough oxygen. He had to pull himself together. He was going down there.

"Young Park," he forced out. "United States Navy SEALs. We're here to rescue you!"

Young looked up from the bottom of the pit. "Help me," he said weakly.

Beanpole and Psycho attached two rappelling ropes to the well, and Chris checked Beanpole's before hooking in. Meanwhile, the other SEALs lay in a perimeter around them, taking cover in a ditch, behind a tractor and whatever else was available. They created the blocking force for anyone who might disturb the rescue.

"Stand against the wall, Young," Chris said. "I'm coming down." The SEALs' powerful HK416 5.56-caliber rounds cracked the night. Enemy AK-47s staccatoed the air, but the noise became muffled as Chris rappelled into the well—his teammates would take care of the insurgents.

Before Chris reached the bottom, the stench hit him with the force of a cargo ship at full speed. His feet touched the ground, and he immediately put a rappelling harness on Young. Part of the offensive odor came from Young: a mixture of urine, feces, and something else Chris couldn't discern. He gagged. Young was missing both ears and most of an arm. In that moment, the wounds were Chris's, and he wanted to kill Mordet.

He attached Young's harness to the free rope and gave it a tug. Chris's teammates pulled Young up. Fortunately, the harness didn't require two hands for balance. Then Chris tugged on his own rope, but there was no response. "Hey, pull me up!"

Chris tugged again, harder. Nothing. "Get me the hell out of here!" Not waiting for an answer, he pulled himself up the rope. He climbed higher and higher—faster and faster. Soon he cleared the top, freed himself from the rope, and took cover behind the well. Oxygen rushed into his lungs like a roaring river.

Psycho grinned with bloodlust with each insurgent he dropped—he enjoyed the killing too much. Beside Chris lay Beanpole, his neck and face covered in liquid goo—he'd been shot. Chris neither liked nor respected Beanpole, but he was still a teammate, and it sucked some of the life out of Chris to see him injured like that. While Little Doc tried to help Beanpole, Young crouched next to them shaking.

Chris dropped the rappelling gear, stood between Young and the enemy, aimed at the nearest attacker, and squeezed the trigger—two to the chest. The attacker landed on his back with his leg folded underneath him. Chris patted Young on the shoulder. "You're going home tonight. You're going to be okay." It's what Chris would want to hear, and it's what Chris intended to deliver.

"Thank you, thank you. I'm going home, I'm going home." He kept repeating his thanks and that he was going home.

Now the whole inland area seemed to move toward them—there must've been nearly a hundred tangos out there, outnumbering the SEALs seven-to-one. Despite his team's talent, the odds favored a SEAL slaughter. If they tried to break contact now, the enemy would overrun them. The

SEALs would have to put up a ferocious fight in order to give the enemy enough pause to allow the frogmen to flee.

The enemy raised the volume of their fire to forte fortissimo and advanced on the SEALs. Chris shot a barrel-chested tango, busting his barrel. Another tango stepped in front of Barrel Chest to take his place. There seemed to be no end to them. The air around Chris cracked off like firecrackers, and a round hit him in the gut, punching the air from his lungs. He gasped for air and said a silent prayer of thanks that the bullet-resistant vest *had* stopped the projectile before it cut into his flesh.

The enemy advanced. Despite the SEALs' best efforts, they couldn't slow the assault.

So this is how it ends.

His promise to get Young home had become a lie.

"Mary Poppins, Sierra One." LT's radioman spoke their call sign anxiously over the communications net, trying to get in touch with a plane above for backup. "Identify our position, over."

"Sierra One, Mary Poppins, I identify fifteen friendlies, over," a crew member on board replied. Flying at an altitude of nearly a mile in the sky, out of enemy small arms and RPG range but within the plane's own artillery and cannons' range, Mary Poppins flew in a wide circle around the battlefield.

"That is correct," LT's radioman confirmed. "Kill everything west of us outside danger close!"

"Roger, Sierra One. Kill everything west of you outside danger close."

Over the noise of the ground fighting, a small clap of thunder came from the sky. The first 105-millimeter, thirty-three-pound projectile popped the sound barrier as it shot to earth. In the middle of the enemies' position, the earth exploded, flinging body parts and dirt. The closest survivors lay stunned in a column of rising smoke.

Six seconds later, the smoke cleared, and another 105-millimeter bomb struck the earth, this time on the enemies' left flank. Most of the insurgents on the right flank figured out it was time to haul booty. Six seconds later, the right flank detonated, obliterating the slow learners.

Meanwhile, the plane's cannon opened up. Each second, two explosive pom-poms blasted clusters of bad guys.

Enemy bullets stopped popping the air around Chris's head.

"Pop smoke," LT commanded over the radio.

Psycho and the rear security SEAL from LT's squad popped their smoke grenades. Soon the smoke blocked the line of sight between the insurgents and the SEALs.

"Leapfrog back to the primary extract," LT said. "Second squad, to the helos."

Chris pulled Young up from the ground. "Run to the chopper!" Chris shouted.

Young didn't have to be told twice. He ran with Chris's squad to the Black Hawk and didn't stop until they arrived safely inside. Doc attended to Beanpole, who was still alive.

Two or three AKs broke out on full auto behind them, but LT's squad silenced them.

"First squad, back," called LT. LT and his teammates rose and dashed to the helo. The AC-130 overhead continued to pound the terrorists with 40 mike-mikes.

Immediately after the rest of the men loaded onto the helos, they lifted off the ground. They flew with the doors open because that was the quickest way to enter and exit, especially during emergencies. The helos turned east and pulled forward. "RPG, six o'clock!" a voice came from the rear of Chris's helo.

"RPG, six o'clock!" others in the middle of the chopper echoed.

"RPG, six o'clock," the pilot acknowledged. He banked the helicopter hard and turned south.

Gravity pulled mercilessly on Chris, and somebody bumped into him, almost knocking him off his bench. It was Young: unable to hold on with one arm, his feet slid out the door and kicked Chris. He had remembered to connect a tether to Young, securing him to the helo, but in all the excitement, he couldn't remember if he'd secured himself.

Chris strained to hug the helo, but gravity continued to pull at him, and the wind continued to whip his body mercilessly. He was losing his own grip. *If I can hold out just a little longer—until the RPG passes and the helo straightens out.*

Boom! The RPG blew up, shaking the helo. Chris slipped. His heart leaped just before Psycho caught him, stopping him from falling off.

The Black Hawk leveled off, and Chris no longer had to fight with gravity. He noticed that he had attached his tether.

He looked around and was glad to see that no one appeared injured. Now they were in the homestretch. More importantly, Young was free. Chris exhaled long and hard.

Psycho put his mouth close to Chris's ear and shouted above the wind, "When we get back, are you really going to give Mordet that piece of your ear?!"

"Are you on meth?"

"It wouldn't be very reverend-like of you to break a promise!"

"Mordet can eat my badonkadonk!"

Psycho laughed. "Be careful what you wish for!"

"I'm finished!"

"What do you mean?" Psycho asked.

"I mean I'm finished with this shit! I'm not going to re-up!" The words came out of his mouth so naturally. It was what he had to do.

Psycho's face became serious. "Really? What are you going to do?"

TO CONTINUE...

To continue Chris's story and get your sample of *Trident's First Gleaming*, just visit Steve's official website here: http://stephentemplin.com.

Since elementary school, Stephen Templin felt a need to write, dreaming of becoming a novelist. Today, he is a *New York Times* and international best-selling author, with the movie rights to one of his books purchased by Vin Diesel. Steve's work has been translated into thirteen languages. He is a "hybrid" author who maintains active book contracts with top publishers such as Simon and Schuster and St. Martin's Press, while also publishing independently.

After high school, he completed Hell Week, qualified as a pistol and rifle expert, blew up things, and practiced small unit tactics during Basic Underwater Demolition/SEAL training. Later, Steve left the navy and became a missionary. He earned his PhD in education, and for fourteen years he lectured as a tenured professor at Meio University in Japan, where he also practiced the martial art aikido. Currently, he lives in the Dallas–Fort Worth area.

To connect with Steve and for updates about new releases, as well as exclusive promotions, visit his website at www.stephentemplin.com.

Made in United States
North Haven, CT
12 August 2022